# English Men of Letters

### EDITED BY JOHN MORLEY

# DE QUINCEY

# DE QUINCEY

BY

## DAVID MASSON

London

MACMILLAN AND CO., Limited

NEW YORK: THE MACMILLAN COMPANY

1902

First Edition 1881
Reprinted 1885
New Issue 1888, 1902

# PREFATORY NOTE.

For matters of fact in the following pages the chief authorities are the collective edition of De Quincey's works in sixteen volumes, published by Messrs. A. & C. Black of Edinburgh, and the Life of De Quincey in two volumes by Mr. H. A. Page (London, John Hogg & Co., 1877). This last, the only extensive and complete Life of De Quincey in the language, contains a large quantity of biographical information supplied to Mr. Page by the family of De Quincey, and by friends and correspondents of his, much of it in the form of interesting letters and papers never before made public. Such information had long been desired in vain; and till the appearance of Mr. Page's work little more was known about De Quincey's life than had been revealed by himself in the autobiographical portions of his writings. While, however, Mr. Page's work and those autobiographical writings of De Quincey have been the main authorities for facts and dates, there have been miscellaneous gleanings from other quarters. The chronological list of De Quincey's magazine-writings drawn up by Mr. H. G. Bohn, and inserted in the article "Quincey, De" in his edition of Lowndes's Bibliographer's Manual, has been of much use; and among smaller memoirs consulted I may mention the article on De Quincey in the current edition of the Encyclopædia Britannica, written by Mr. J. R. Findlay, one of the most intimate friends of De Quincey in his last years. At various points a little independent research has been found necessary, chiefly in the form of an inspection of the old volumes of the magazines and other periodicals in which De Quincey's papers originally appeared. For the rest, I have some advantage in having myself met and conversed with De Quincey, so as to retain a perfect recollection of his appearance, voice, and manner, and in being familiar with the scenes amid which he spent the last nine-and-twenty years of his life.

EDINBURGH,
    *August*, 1881.

# CONTENTS.

## CHAPTER VIII.

## CHAPTER IX.

## CHAPTER X.

## CHAPTER XI.

## CHAPTER XII.

# DE QUINCEY.

## CHAPTER I.

DE QUINCEY took some pains to explain that his family
was not, as the form of the name might suggest, a recent
French importation into England, but had come in with
the Conquest. Genealogists, indeed, find that the first of
the English De Quinceys was a certain companion of the
Conqueror, named Richard, probably of Norwegian descent,
though hailing more immediately from the village or district of Quincé in French Normandy. His descendants
became great personages in England, reaching their highest
in one or two De Quinceys who were Earls of Winchester
in the thirteenth century. De Quincey, while dwelling
with fondness on these associations with his name, admits
that the Earls of Winchester and their shadowy crusading
retinue " suddenly came to grief," and that most of the
English De Quinceys for many generations before his own
time had been very insignificant and obscure persons.
With other English families of like origin, they had
dropt the aristocratic prefix *De ;* in addition to which

B

they had consented, in the easy old days of optional spelling, to be *Quincys* or *Quincies* or *Quinceys*, just as it might please their neighbours.

It seems to have been De Quincey himself, though he does not mention the matter, who resuscitated the prefix *De* (which he always wrote, however, with the small *d* and not with the capital) in his particular branch of the family. His father, at all events, called himself Thomas Quincey. This father of De Quincey must have been a rather interesting man. He is described by his son as having been " literary to the extent of having written a book ;" which book has been identified by very recent research with an anonymous octavo volume or pamphlet published in London in 1775, and entitled *A Short Tour in the Midland Counties of England, performed in the Summer of* 1772 : *together with an Account of a Similar Excursion undertaken September* 1774. The greater part of the contents of the volume had previously appeared in five successive instalments in the *Gentleman's Magazine* for May, June, July, August, and September, 1774, under the title " A Tour in the Midland Counties of England, performed in the summer of 1772. (By T—— Q——) ;" and the separate publication, as a preface explains, was occasioned partly by the author's resentment of the liberties that had been taken with the original text by the editor of the magazine, and partly by a desire to improve the piece into " a less soporific potion for the mental taste of his friends." Though in the form of brief business-like notes, the performance is altogether very creditable. The jottings give the author's observations of the state of farming, draining, manufactures, mining industry, &c., in the district traversed, with hints of decided opinions of his own on several vexed economic questions. There is

an eye also for the picturesque in scenery, and for archi-
tectural beauties or defects in towns, churches, and country
seats ; and the style is that of a well-educated man, accustomed to write English.   Once or twice the language rises
towards the poetic, and once there is an admiring quotation from Beattie's *Minstrel*, the first part of which had
recently appeared.   At the time of this first and only
literary venture of De Quincey's father he cannot have
been more than three-and-twenty years of age ; and one
infers, from the matter of the performance, that he was
then residing in London, in some commercial occupation
which took him occasionally on a circuit northwards.
There is a suggestion of previous acquaintance with
Lincolnshire, and of some special connexion with that
county.   There would be little difficulty, we suppose, in
investigating these antecedents of the interesting T. Q.
of 1774 ; meanwhile what concerns us here is that
within about five years from that date he is found settled
in Manchester as a rising merchant, with his town-house
or place of business in Fountain Street, and with extensive
transactions and correspondence, especially with Portugal,
America, and the West Indies.   He had then married a
Miss Penson, a lady of very good family connexions, two
brothers of whom, younger than herself, went out soon
afterwards to Bengal as officers in the service of the East
India Company.   Of this marriage there were born,
between 1779 and 1792, eight children in all, four of them
sons and four daughters.   Our De Quincey, the fifth
child and the second son, was born on the 15th of August,
1785, when his father was about thirty-three years of age,
and his mother about three years younger.

The memoirs of De Quincey have been wonderfully
unanimous in the statement that he was born at a country

house of his father's, called Greenhay, in what was then
a perfectly rustic neighbourhood, about a mile out of
Manchester. The statement is a blunder. De Quincey
himself distinctly informs us that he was born *in* Manchester, though he passed the whole of his childhood, after
the first few weeks of his existence, in a rural seclusion
near the town. He informs us further that this suburban
seclusion, the habitual abode of the family after his birth,
as distinct from the town-house or place of business which
his father continued to keep up in Fountain Street, was
first in "a pretty rustic dwelling" called *The Farm*, and
not till about 1791 or 1792 in the larger country-house of
*Greenhay*, which his father had then just built and
equipped at an expense of about 6000*l.* The name
*Greenhay*, he adds, was then an invention of his mother's,
partly in recognition of the vicinity of a hamlet called
Greenhill, and partly to signify, by revival of the old
English word *hay*, meaning hedge or hedge-row (same as
the French *haie*), that the domicile was characteristically
a country mansion, with lawns and gardens, sequestered
within gates and a verdant ring-fence. The priority of
"The Farm" to "Greenhay" is indubitable.

In the life of De Quincey even such a trifle is worth
noting. In no autobiography do the recollections of
mere infancy and childhood occupy so much space, or
count for so much, as in his. Accordingly, while the
general impression he conveys of himself from his second
or third year onwards is that of a very diminutive, shy,
sensitive, and dreamy child, moving about, when out of
doors, always on green turf or in garden-walks, and within doors always among young brothers and sisters in a
house of wealthy and even luxurious elegance, the
actual incidents of his infancy and childhood which he

has embalmed for us so carefully in such marvellous prose
have to be distributed between the two habitations above
named, once visible on the rustic margin of Manchester,
but now engulfed in its brick and uproar. It was at
"The Farm" that he had the "remarkable dream of terrific
grandeur about a favourite nurse," which proved to him
afterwards that his dreaming tendencies had been constitutional; it was here that the first sense of pathos had come
over him, in watching, very early in spring, the appearance
of some crocuses; and it was here that he had his first
experiences of death in a household. Of his three sisters
older than himself, Jane, the second in age, died before
he was two years old; and he could remember the whisper
that ran through the house, muffled so as not to reach his
mother, of some harsh treatment of the dying sufferer by
one of the female servants. Then, four years later, came
the death of the eldest sister, Elizabeth, the gentlest and
best beloved, his instructress and constant companion,
whose image, and the signs of whose noble intellectual
promise in her face and forehead, though she had not
attained her tenth year, were to dwell with him, like a
visionary guardianship from the spiritual world, through
all the future years of his own life. Who can forget the
pages in which he tells of the trance of reverie and
delirium which fell upon him that bright midsummer day,
when he had stolen alone into the chamber where the
little corpse lay, and, in the flood of sunshine that streamed
into the chamber from the cloudless sky without, there
seemed suddenly to moan forth a solemn wind, "a wind
that might have swept the fields of mortality for a thousand centuries," rising and swelling till the eye partook of
the magic of the ear, and the billows of unearthly music
seemed to tend to a shaft that ran upwards in quest of

the throne of God? All these incidents, in their literal original, or in the transfiguration given to them by poetic memory, have to be referred to the period when "Greenhay" was yet to come ; and, when we do enter that house, in the year 1792, it is with the knowledge of a new fact in the family history. De Quincey, then in his seventh year, had seen, he tells us, so little of his father that, if the two had met anywhere by chance, they would not have known each other. The merchant, though in the prime of his manhood, had long been the prey of a pulmonary consumption ; and for several years he had been in the habit, for the benefit of his health, while attending to his foreign and colonial business transactions, of residing as much as possible in Lisbon or Madeira, or in some of the West India Islands, with but occasional visits to England. But, one day, when the house of Greenhay was still somewhat of a novelty, and the mother had gone to meet her invalid husband at the port where he was expected, it was known to the children that their father was coming home. He was coming home, in fact, to die. For hours, in the summer evening, the children and servants had been on the lawn before the house, listening for the sound of wheels in the winding lane that led from the main road ; and it was not till near midnight that the horses' heads emerged from the gloom, the carriage then approaching the house at a hearse-like pace, and the white pillows on which the invalid was propped catching the eye of the child and striking his imagination with a ghastly effect. For several weeks the invalid languished on a sofa, his quietest and most dreamy child admitted to him in his waking hours more than the rest, and standing beside him with the rest when he died.

By the father's death, the family, consisting of the

mother and six children, the last posthumously born, was
left poorer than it had been, but still in clear possession
of 1600*l.* a year. The allowance for each of the four sons
was to be 150*l.* a year, and that for each of the two surviving daughters 100*l.* a year, while the rest seems to
have been left at the disposal of the mother. In the
guardianship of the children till they came of age there
were associated with the mother four selected friends of
the father, living in or near Manchester; but the real
management for the time was with the mother. De
Quincey's mentions of his mother are uniformly respectful
and reverent, with just a shade of critical remark on that
side of her character which ruled her relations to himself.
Of stately social ways and refined tastes, and of even
rare natural endowments, she was, De Quincey says,
though in no sense professedly a *literary* woman, yet
emphatically "an *intellectual* woman," whose letters
among her friends, if they could have been collected and
published, would have been found hardly inferior, for the
racy grace of their idiomatic English, to those of Lady
Mary Wortley Montagu. But there was, he hints, a
touch too much of Roman firmness or hardness in her,
which, especially after her friendship with Hannah More
and other notables of the Clapham Evangelical Sect had
confirmed her in their rigid views of religion, disqualified
her for the peculiarly sympathetic treatment required by
at least one of her sons. The present writer knew a
venerable lady who, in her youth, had seen much of De
Quincey's mother; and her account tallied closely with
De Quincey's own. Indeed, this venerable lady, being
herself a strict religionist of the antique evangelical type,
retained to the last an opinion of De Quincey which she
had probably caught from colloquies with his mother con-

cerning him in his most dubious days. A stately woman, every inch a lady, moving in the best county circles, and with her feet on the Rock of Ages,—such was, and always had been, De Quincey's mother; as for the son, celebrity or no celebrity, what was he but a waif?

For four years after the death of De Quincey's father, or from 1792 to 1796, the widow continued to live at Greenhay, with her orphan children about her, doing her best for their education. We hardly know when De Quincey began to read and write; but, from all he tells us of the years of his life that have now been sketched, one infers that, with perhaps too little music or other kindred recreation in the house, reading had been absolutely unrestricted for him and his sisters, and that he had been always with one of them when he could, or in a quiet corner by himself, conning some delicious piece of juvenile verse or prose. Dr. Johnson and Cowper were then the English authors of greatest recent repute; but, in addition to the Bible, it is of Mrs. Barbauld's books and the *Arabian Nights* that we hear as first fascinating the De Quincey children and moving them to questions. In one very suggestive chapter, treating of the power of individual passages in books to find out the minds fitted for their reception, De Quincey cites as an instance in his own case the effect upon him, in his childhood, of the opening passage in the story of Aladdin. That there should be a magician dwelling in the depths of Africa, and aware of an enchanted lamp, imprisoned somewhere in a subterranean chamber, which could be found out only by the child predestined for the adventure, and that this magician, by putting his ear to the ground and listening to the sounds of the footsteps of all the human beings living on the globe, should know for certain that the

predestined finder of the lamp was a little boy then
running about, thousands of miles off, in the streets of
Bagdad, was a revelation of the universal connexions of
things which gave rise to no end of pondering. This
from the *Arabian Nights*, and an anecdote of noble
revenge picked out of a historical miscellany, were, we are
given to understand, the passages of literature that had
fastened most strongly on the little De Quincey at the
time when his sister Elizabeth was still alive to share his
enthusiasms. At the date at which we have now arrived,
however, there was a change of circumstances. The boy
had come to an age when home-teaching and miscellaneous
voluntary reading were to be supplemented by something
more regular, in the shape of daily lessons under a tutor
conveniently near. The tutor chosen was the Rev. S. H.,
one of the guardians of the children by their father's will,
and then curate of a church in the part of Manchester
called Salford. To the house of this Mr. S. H., about
two miles from Greenhay, the little fellow was to trudge
daily for his lessons in the morning, returning in the
afternoon. This would not have mattered much if he had
remained still the eldest boy in the Greenhay household.
But, since the father's death, there had come to live at
Greenhay, and to partake in the lessons from Mr. S H. at
Salford, Master William De Quincey himself, the very
top of the family, full twelve years of age, or about five
years older than Thomas. Hitherto Thomas had known
little or nothing of this senior brother of his, who had
been for some time with his father in Lisbon, and then,
proving unmanageable, had been sent to the Grammar
School of Louth in Lincolnshire. But now he was to
know enough. Never was such a boy as this William
De Quincey, such a boisterous, frank, pugilistic, clever,

inventive, not unlikeable, but wholly unendurable, son of eternal racket. " His genius for mischief amounted to inspiration," reports his principal victim. For no sooner had he arrived than he had taken possession of the house and all in it like a whirlwind, and poor little Thomas, as the next living thing under him, had been collared by him at once for his fag and spaniel.

It is not for nothing that De Quincey heads the long chapter of more than eighty pages in which he treats of the time of his subjection to the despotism of his stormy elder brother with the words *Introduction to the World of Strife.* Digressive as that chapter is, one receives from it a unity of general impression corresponding to the title. One can see that, during the three years and a half of which so much fun is made in the retrospect, the nervous little creature who had been linked to such a steam-engine of a brother was in the main very miserable. It was not merely that his brother had picked a quarrel with the boys of a cotton-factory on the skirts of Manchester, just at the point where the road from Greenhay entered the town by a particular bridge, and that once or twice every day, as they went and came between Greenhay and their tutor's house in Salford, there had to be a battle at this spot between them and some of the factory-boys, every recurrence of which threw the little creature into new terror. It was that his very thoughts and imaginations were no longer his own, but were dictated to him and shaped for him by the energies of his companion. The war with the factory-boys itself, for example, became a double torment by being idealized by his brother into a great enterprise in which he was commander-in-chief, with absolute powers, while Thomas was the responsible second. For his conduct in the campaign from day to day in this character

of responsible second was not only incessantly discussed
by the commander-in-chief in their colloquies along the
road, but was the subject of merciless comment in bulletins
and gazettes published by the commander-in-chief for the
benefit of Mrs. Evans, the housekeeper at Greenhay, and
the rest of the world there.   Now he was promoted to be
major-general, as having done pretty well; now he was
under arrest for cowardice and was to be drummed out of
the army; again, restored to his rank by the intercession
of a distinguished lady (Mrs. Evans), he received also the
Order of the Bath; and once he was in danger of being
hanged for treacherous correspondence with the enemy.
Nor was this all.   Besides being commander-in-chief in
the war with the factory-boys, his brother was king of an
imaginary kingdom called Tigrosylvania; and poor De
Quincey, to accommodate him in his Napoleonic pro-
pensities to invasion, was obliged to be king of another
imaginary kingdom called Gombroon.   Then not only
was Gombroon liable to invasion by the Tigrosylvanians,
but the wretched government of Gombroon and the low
state of civilization among the Gombroonians became a
subject of perpetual sarcasm on the part of the Tigro-
sylvanian monarch.   The lowest depth of De Quincey's
degradation in the matter was when his brother, having
been reading an extract from Monboddo, informed him
gravely that he had ascertained that the Gombroonians
were still in the primitive condition of mankind, not
having advanced so far as even to acquire those sedentary
habits the continuance of which through ages would
remove their tails, and advised him to issue an edict
requiring them all to sit for at least six hours every day,—
which, he said, though it could not do much, would make
a beginning.   It was the same in all the other relations

between the imperious young sultan of the family and his
junior brothers and sisters. In his pyrotechnics for their
amusement, his lectures to them on chemistry and natural
philosophy, his dramatic recitations, he was always lord-
paramount, and they were his thralls. Of De Quincey
himself his opinion, frankly intimated from the first, was
that he was physically contemptible, and mentally an idiot,
though with some good moral qualities. Of the truth of
this opinion, communicated so authoritatively, De Quincey
says he had at first no doubt. It coincided with that idea
of himself into which he had settled in those moping days
of childish melancholy and reverie which his brother's
arrival in Greenhay had disturbed ; and he would have
been only too glad if " that solid foundation of utter
despicableness " to which he had learned to trust had
been left unshaken. On the whole, he thinks, it was
perhaps well that it was shaken. Left to himself with
his other young brothers and sisters, he might have moped
on till the taint of consumption had been developed in
him ; and his vehement elder brother's discipline had acted
as a rough febrifuge.

Meanwhile the lessons with the Rev. Mr. S. H. had
been sufficiently profitable. A conscientious man, though
decidedly dull, he had grounded De Quincey well in
Latin, and entered him in Greek ; and there had been,
moreover, a special excrescence from the tutorship, which,
though irksome, had been beneficial. Mr. H. had a
stock of three hundred and thirty sermons, each about
sixteen minutes long, which, at the rate of two sermons
every Sunday, served as spiritual nutriment for his con-
gregation for a cycle of three years. The De Quincey
family having to come in their carriage from Greenhay to
church, it was only the forenoon sermon that the boy

heard; but of this he was expected regularly to give in a correct abstract in the course of the week. As the tutor did not allow notes to be taken, the exercise of memory was of lasting benefit. To these results of the tutorship add the results of the continued readings of the boy through the three years and a half, whether in connexion with the lessons or independently. As before, he dwells on individual passages that had impressed him. One passage that sank into him with a mystic sense of power was the phrase in the book of Daniel, "Belshazzar the king made a great feast to a thousand of his lords." Another instance is even more remarkable. No reader of De Quincey but must have observed how frequent and important a word in his vocabulary is the word *Pariah*, meaning "social outcast," and what a hold had been taken of his imagination by the idea that an immense proportion of the men and women of the world, in all ages and all lands, had belonged to the class of *Pariahs*, the socially outcast for one reason or another, the despised, the unrespectable, the maltreated and downtrodden. Well, this idea, if his own dating is to be trusted, had been fixed in him irrevocably even in the present early period of his life. It was implanted in him first by the ineffable feeling of sublimity which he attached to those lines in the Epilogue to the second book of the Fables of Phædrus where that Latin fabulist, who had himself been a slave, exulted in the recollection that his predecessor, the Greek slave Æsop, had triumphed by his genius over the circumstances of his birth:—

> Æsopi ingenio statuam posuere Attici,
> Servumque collocarunt æterna in basi,
> Patere honoris scirent ut cunctis viam,
> Nec generi tribui sed virtuti gloriam.[1]

---

[1] De Quincey quotes only the first two lines of these four

But it was not from this passage alone, nor from mere
literature, that he derived the idea in its full extension.
It chanced that in the house of a certain reverend gentleman there were two twin girls, his daughters, who were
deaf and scrofulous and reputed to be all but idiots, and
whom therefore their mother, ashamed of them and dis-
liking them, kept as much out of sight as possible, using
them as menial drudges, and cruel to them otherwise,
while the father, whatever he may have thought, did not
interfere.  The acute boy, prying about the house, and
coming to know and pity the girls, had laid the case to
heart.  Were not these girls also *Pariahs*, and were there
not other concealed varieties of *Pariahs* in Christian
England?

It had been arranged by the guardians that the elder
brother, who had shown a talent for drawing, should go
into training for the profession of an artist by becoming
pupil to the distinguished London landscape-painter and
Royal Academician, De Loutherbourg.  As the parting
with his brother was to be a new starting-point in De
Quincey's life, he remembered it well, the more by token
of an incident of the very last morning of his brother's
stay at Greenhay.  It was a splendid June morning before
breakfast, and all the six children were together in the
grounds in front of the house, from Sultan William, now
in his sixteenth year, down to the youngest.  William
was full of frolic, with the two girls laughing and dancing
beside him, and the baby Henry near in the nurse's arms;

translating them " *A colossal statue did the Athenians raise to
Æsop, and a poor pariah slave they planted upon an everlasting
pedestal* "  The rest may run " *This they did in acknowledgment
of the fact that the path of honour is open to all, and that glory
belongs not to birth but to worth.*"

Richard, called familiarly " Pink," the next to De Quincey
in age, was wheeling round on his heel at some distance ;
while De Quincey himself was standing close to the edge
of a brook which bounded the grounds on that part
where they were not protected from the lane by a railing
and the gates. Suddenly there was a vast uproar in the
lane, the noise of a shouting and running mob coming
nearer and nearer, explained at last by the appearance of
a great dog, much ahead of his pursuers, and panting and
foaming at the mouth. The dog tried the gates, which
were fortunately shut ; then stood for a moment on the
edge of the brook directly opposite to De Quincey, as if
meditating a leap across ; and then, amid the scare of the
children, all except the intrepid William, who taunted and
challenged the dog to come over, broke away again along
the lane, followed by the long hullabaloo of men and boys,
with guns, sticks, and pitchforks. It was a mad dog
from a barracks, which had already that morning bitten
two horses. He led his pursuers a chase of many miles
before he was killed. One of the two horses he had bitten
died afterwards of hydrophobia. What if he had leaped
the brook ?

# CHAPTER II.

SOME time in 1796, De Quincey's mother having made up
her mind to live at Bath, the establishment at Greenhay
was broken up, and the house and grounds were sold.
After being boarded for a while in Manchester, for continuation of the lessons under Mr. S. H., De Quincey
followed his mother to Bath, and was entered at the
Grammar School of the town, then presided over by a
Mr. Morgan, an excellent classical scholar. He was then
in his twelfth year, and was to have as one of his schoolfellows his brother Richard, already mentioned by his
nickname of "Pink," about four years younger than himself, and a boy of exquisite beauty, and of a sweet gentleness that made him the most absolute contrast to the
terrible William. Of that young hurricane and all his
problematical capabilities De Quincey had seen the last.
He died of typhus fever soon after he had become pupil
to the Academician De Loutherbourg.

De Quincey remained at the Bath Grammar School
about two years. From the first he had the reputation
of a little prodigy in it, especially in Latin, and most
especially for Latin verse-making. In this accomplishment
he had such success that the head-master used to parade

his exercises publicly by way of reproach to the stiff Latinity of the boys of the first form, most of whom were five or six years older. On the other hand, he was at first somewhat backward in Greek,—on which account he had been placed under the second of the Bath School masters, rather than with the more advanced boys under Mr. Morgan himself. For some time there was a cabal among these advanced boys against the little interloper who was snatching from them the honours in Latin. On the whole, however, he was comfortable enough, and was rapidly attaining an unusual facility in speaking and writing Greek, when an accident led to his removal from the school. The most exact account of this accident is found in a boyish letter of his own, which chances to have survived. It is dated March 12, 1799, and was addressed to his sister Mary, then at a school in Bristol. " This day six weeks," are his words, " as we were up saying " [repeating our lessons], Mr. M. was called out, and so " forsooth little, or rather *big*, Mounseer Collins [one of " the undermasters] must jump into the desk. It hap- " pened that little Harman minor wanted his hat, which " hung up over Collins' head. Wilbraham asked for the " cane to reach it him, which Collins refused ; and at the " same time, to give a little strength, I suppose, to his " refusal, and to enforce his authority as a master, en- " deavoured to hit him on the shoulder (as *he* says) : but " how shall I relate the sequel ? On poor Ego did it fall. " Say, Muse, what could inspire the cane with such a dire- " ful purpose ? But not on my shoulder, on my *pate*, it " fell,—unhappy pate, worthy of a better fate ! " The blow on the head, thus playfully described, seemed serious at the time. For some weeks De Quincey lay in his mother's house in Bath, attended by physicians and under

severe regimen. In the weeks of his gradual recovery his
mother read to him steadily till he could resume reading
for himself. Among the books thus read he mentions
Sir William Jones's *Asiatic Researches*, Milner's *Church
History*, Johnson's *Rambler*, Hoole's *Translations of
Ariosto and Tasso*, with the notable addition of *Paradise
Lost*, which had come to him, strangely enough, in Bentley's grotesque edition. At the same time he and his
brother Pink had lessons in French.

Although the head-master and others interested in Bath
Grammar School tried to get back their little prodigy, the
mother would not consent. She sent him and his brother
Pink to a private school at Winkfield, in Wiltshire, " of
which the chief recommendation lay in the religious
character of the master." Here he remained about a year,
not thinking much of " old Spencer," the master, but a
great favourite with the Miss Spencers, and with the thirty
or forty boarders. Fifty years afterwards, two of his
schoolfellows, clergymen of the Church of England, could
remember him at Spencer's as a most obliging and com-
panionable little fellow, willing to help any of the boys in
their Latin or Greek, and a leader in their amusements, to
which he would always give a literary turn. He divided
the boys for their mimic fights into Greeks and Trojans,
taking the part of Ulysses himself ; and, in his capacity of
contributor-in-chief to a journal carried on by the boys
and the Miss Spencers, he replied in pungent English
verses to a challenge by the boys of a neighbouring school.
It was remembered also that, when his mother came to
visit the school, and the boys talked of her as a friend of
Hannah More, he would tell them with pride that his
mother was quite as clever as Hannah.

Hardly more than a year had been spent at Winkfield

when the connexion with that school was brought to an end by an invitation to De Quincey of a kind which his mother did not see fit to refuse. During the time of the convalescence at Bath, in the spring of 1799, an acquaintance had sprung up between De Quincey and young Lord Westport, the only child of John-Denis, third Earl of Altamont of the Irish peerage, afterwards Marquis of Sligo. The boy, whom De Quincey represents as almost exactly of his own age, but whom the peerage books represent as considerably younger, had been then in the neighbourhood of Bath, with his tutor, Mr. Grace. He and his tutor had been asked to Mrs. De Quincey's house; and now, after more than a year, during which his young lordship had been at Eton, there came the invitation we speak of. It was an invitation to join Lord Westport at Eton and accompany him in a long holiday on his father's estates in county Mayo in the West of Ireland. Arrangements having been duly made, De Quincey did set out for Eton in the summer of 1800, to begin a ramble and round of visits in England and Ireland, which extended over four or five months.

Eton itself was a good beginning. That classic town, as all the world ought to know, is really part and parcel of Windsor, within whose royal precincts is Frogmore, a seat of royalty subsidiary to Windsor Castle. Now, as George III. and his Queen, with the princesses, were at Frogmore in the summer of 1800, and as Lord Westport not only had the run of Frogmore grounds, but was specially known to the royal family, as the son and heir-apparent of the Earl of Altamont, and as grandson by his mother of the lately deceased Earl Howe, the famous Admiral, what was to prevent De Quincey, in such good company, from having an interview with his

Majesty himself? This, he tells us, actually occurred.
The King, recognizing Lord Westport in one of the
Frogmore walks, stopped him and talked with him a
little, and then, turning to his companion, whose name
he had somehow already heard, asked whether he too
was at Eton, and whether his father was alive, and
whether his mother thought of sending him to Eton,—a
capital school, none better!—and whether his family was
of French Huguenot descent. To all which De Quincey
returned, he says, brief and modest answers, only throwing
a little energy into his repudiation of any recent French
origin, and informing his Majesty that the English De
Quinceys were as old as the Conquest, and were mentioned in the very earliest of English books, Robert of
Gloucester's *Metrical Chronicle*. "I know, I know," said
the King with a smile, as if he remembered such a book
in his library, but did not like to commit himself on
the subject with such a knowing little shrimp; and the
interview ended, the two boys stepping backward a few
paces and bowing profoundly, while his Majesty moved
away. This, however, was not De Quincey's last sight
of the King. He had the honour of being invited, with
Lord Westport, to one or two of the *fêtes* which the
Queen was then giving at Frogmore, and did attend one
of them,—in a travelling dress, as his mother heard with
horror, till he explained to her in a letter that his travel-
ling-dress was a very good one, "much better than what
Lord Westport had on," and that in such a crush it
did not matter. The stay at Eton was broken by a run
to London. It was De Quincey's first sight of the great
metropolis, and he is punctual in dating it as in the
month of May.

From Eton, where De Quincey, as he informed his mother

very penitentially, could not avoid going once to a
play in Windsor Theatre to oblige Lord Westport, the
two lads, with the tutor, began their journey for Ireland
on the 18th of July. Travelling through North Wales,
they reached Holyhead, where the tutor was to leave
them. At that place the tutor, who had taken mysterious
offence at something or other, and apparently begun to
have doubts about De Quincey, ceased to speak with
either of the lads, but duly saw them aboard the packet
that was to take them to Dublin. The passage of thirty
hours, the arrival in Dublin, the first impressions of that
city, and the various incidents and pleasures of the fortnight or so passed there, are described at considerable
length in the subsequent autobiographic record. It was
an unusually interesting time in the History of Ireland,
for it was the time of the completion in the Irish Parliament of the Bill for the Union of Ireland with Great
Britain. Introduced to his friend's father, the Earl of
Altamont, " a very fat man, and so lame that he is obliged
to have two servants to support him whenever he stirs,"
De Quincey had access to all the sights and demonstra-
tions of the crisis. He was present at the splendid cere-
mony of the installation of the Knights of St. Patrick ;
and he was present in the last sittings of the Irish House
of Peers, when the Union Act was passed. He saw the
Lord Lieutenant Cornwallis, Lord and Lady Castlereagh,
and other great public persons ; and he saw the surgings
in the streets of excited Irish mobs. From such personal reminiscences of his Dublin visit he deviates into a
general essay on the social and political state of Ireland
at the time, with particular accounts of the two recent
Irish Rebellions, &c. ; and it is when we are extricated
from these that we find him at last, about the 20th

of August, at Lord Altamont's seat of Westport in Connaught. There, in a big house, with but a slovenly
collection of books in it, but with wild Irish scenery
round about for excursions, wild Irish horses to ride,
and wilder Irish grooms to study, he spent some weeks
pleasantly enough, coaching Lord Westport at odd
moments, it would seem, in Greek and Latin.

One starry experience dwelt with him all the while. In
that part of his journey from Dublin to Connaught which
had been performed on the Grand Canal, leading from
Dublin to Tullamore, there had been among his fellow-
passengers in the canal-boat the widowed Countess of
Errol, in deep mourning, and her sister Miss Blake. Both
ladies were of Irish birth, and both were young, beautiful,
and accomplished. Introduced by Lord Westport, De
Quincey was for a time in Elysium. Mentioning the
rencontre in a letter to his mother at the time, all that
he says is that "in the canal-boat was a Miss Blake, a
sister of the present Countess Dowager of Errol," and that
they "formed an acquaintance and talked about the
English poets for the whole afternoon." It is in the
Autobiography that we learn the whole truth. Miss
Blake, with her soft eyes and soft Irish voice, her Irish
gaiety and affluence in talk, had impressed him as
he had never been impressed before. "From this
day," he says, "I was an altered creature, never again
relapsing into the careless irreflective mind of childhood."

Returning from Ireland to England in October 1800,
the two friends parted at Birmingham; and one observes it as rather curious that Lord Westport is hardly
heard of again in De Quincey's history, whether under
the title of Earl of Altamont, which he could assume by

courtesy before the year closed, in consequence of his
father's promotion to the Marquisate of Sligo, or under
that of Marquis of Sligo, which was his own from 1809
to 1845. Meanwhile we are not quite done with De
Quincey's ramble. From Birmingham, as instructed by a
letter from his mother, he went to Laxton in North-
amptonshire, where his elder sister already was. It was
the seat of Lord and Lady Carbery, the latter of whom, in
her unmarried condition as Miss Watson, a wealthy heiress,
had long been an intimate young friend of his mother's.
A Lord and Lady Massey were also staying at Laxton,
and Lord Carbery himself arrived from Ireland; and, as
there was a fine library in the house, with all the appurtenances of luxurious culture, a month or two of rest in
such English seclusion were very acceptable after so
much rough Irish locomotion. Lady Carbery, a handsome woman of about six and twenty, was abundantly
kind to the boy, both for his mother's sake and his own.
She arranged that he should have daily lessons in riding,
to which he submitted, with no very effective result; she
called him her "Admirable Crichton," and taxed all his
resources of acquired knowledge; and in one department
she became his grateful pupil. Having imbibed the sen-
timents of the Evangelical School of Religion, with
Hannah More and Mrs. De Quincey for her exemplars,
but having a strong and inquiring intellect, she had
begun a systematic study of Theology, and had come to
be vexed by the question whether the authorized
English version of the Bible could be relied on as presenting the exact doctrinal truth on all points. Her
young adviser having assured her that on some points it
could not, she felt as if her salvation might depend on
her having a Greek New Testament and a Parkhurst's

Greek Lexicon beside her; and De Quincey, having encouraged the idea, had the pleasure of setting her agoing in her Greek studies. Altogether he was very happy at Laxton, and there can hardly be a pleasanter picture than that of the high-minded young matron of the mansion, a kind of English variety of Goethe's "Fair Saint," looking after her youthful guest, on the one hand, as a feeble boy that needed superintendence, and on the other hand finding instruction for hours in listening to his suggestive, eloquent, and prematurely learned talk.

The effects upon De Quincey's mind of his long ramble, with the varied glimpses it had given him of the actual world, and especially of an aristocratic section of it, had been, he says, something extraordinary. The rate of his intellectual expansion, he says, was no longer like the movement of the hour hand of a watch, whose advance, though certain, is matter of inference, but was like the visible pace of the seconds' hand. One may question whether a matter-of-fact person would not rather have described the effects of his tour and its incidents as perturbing and unsettling.

Experience seems to have decided that, in the majority of cases, the wisest plan for parents and guardians in the education of a boy is to find out the best established routine of public schooling for boys in his circumstances, and to keep to that inflexibly through all its stages for the usual period. This seems to have been De Quincey's own belief. Of the two schools he had been at he greatly preferred Bath Grammar School; it had been against his will that he had been removed from it; and in his letters to his mother from Ireland he had argued earnestly for a return to that school, if to any, till he should be thought of age for the University. In any

case, he objected to being sent to another private school,
like that at Winkfield. "I was at the head of the
"school the whole time I was there. No one but myself
"could make verses and all those kinds of things; but
"then I had no one to contend with, nor anything higher
"to aspire to. The consequence was that my powers en-
"tirely flagged; my mind became dormant in comparison
"with what it was at the Bath Grammar School." These
remonstrances were so far attended to that, when he left
Lady Carbery's at Laxton, the arrangement of his mother
and guardians was that he should not be sent again to
any private school, but should go for three years to the
Grammar School of his native town of Manchester.
Their chief reason was a pecuniary one. Among the endowments of Manchester Grammar School were certain
exhibitions by which boys who had been regularly at the
school for three full years could be sent to Brasenose
College, Oxford, with 40l. or 50l. a year guaranteed them
for seven years. With 50l. a year added to his patrimonial inheritance of 150l., De Quincey would be able, in
his nineteenth year, to go to Oxford in proper gentlemanly
style, with an annual 200l. for his expenses.

With sighs and forebodings, De Quincey did go to
Manchester Grammar School, some time late in 1800, for
his three years of drudgery. His account of the school,
and of the head master, Mr. Lawson, in whose house he
was boarded, is far from unfriendly on the whole. Mr.
Lawson, though in his declining years, and not quite at
ease with his own head boys in their higher Greek readings, was kind, conscientious, and exemplary; the school
was an ancient and rich one, with historical traditions and
good appliances and accommodations; the discipline was
maintained entirely by moral means, which was rather

rare at that time ; and the boarders, with whom De Quincey had principally to associate, were mostly Lanca- shire youths of good manners and principles, with a col- lective amount of knowledge and ability among them, especially in English literature, which rather surprised the new comer at first. He had a pleasant little room at the top of the house, and books at will by a subscription to the Manchester library. But there were objections. He does not positively include among these the fact that many of the day-boys in the school were sons of artisans, some of them even having " sisters that were menial servants ;" but he mentions the fact ; and he admits generally that the whole atmosphere of Manchester, where he could not stir out of doors without being " nosed by a factory, a cotton-bag, a cotton-dealer, or something else allied to that detestable commerce," had become insuffer- ably uncongenial. It was, however, the monotony of the school life itself that put him out of spirits,—the sight day after day of the same bare white-washed walls, the dull repetition from day to day of petty linguistic tasks that had no stimulus for him now, and were far beneath his capacity. Above all, the total deprivation of physical exercise inflicted on Mr. Lawson's boarders by his absurd system of regulating their hours from morning to evening, with " callings-over " even in the intervals for meals and rest, had a ruinous effect on De Quincey's health. For some time he had been enabled to bear up against the com- plicated miseries by accidental compensations. Lady Car- bery had been in Manchester for some months, with a portion of her household, just after his entry into the new school ; a venerable old clergyman of the town, of Sweden- borgian views, and author of various Swedenborgian tracts, had taken a fancy for the extraordinary lad and his con-

versation, and liked him to call ; and, in one or two runs
to Liverpool, an acquaintance had been struck up with
the club of *literati* of which that town could then boast,
and of which Roscoe, and Dr. Currie, the biographer of
Burns, were the chiefs. But, after a year and a half at
the school, the prospect of another year and a half became
intolerable. In a letter to his mother, still extant, he
pleads most pitifully for his immediate removal. He
enumerates, and emphasises in italic words, his five individual causes of complaint, and then rolls them all in
characteristic fashion into one collective sixth. How could
a person be happy, he asks, or even simply easy, " in a
" situation which deprives him of *health*, of *society*, of
" *amusement*, of *liberty*, of *congeniality of pursuits*, and
" which, to complete the precious picture, admits of no
" *variety ?* " Even this pitiful pleading was of no avail,
and De Quincey was driven to a desperate resolution.
He resolved to run away. After brooding over the
resolution for some time, and procuring the necessary
funds from Lady Carbery, who, knowing nothing of her
young friend's purpose, sent him 10*l.* in answer to his
application by letter for 5*l.*, he carried it into effect by
slipping out of Mr. Lawson's house early one morning in
July 1802. He had an English poet in one pocket, and
an odd volume of Euripides in the other. He was then
close on seventeen years of age.

# CHAPTER III.

DE QUINCEY'S first intention, when he had made up his mind to run away from Manchester School, was to wander towards the district of the English Lakes. The magnet that attracted him thither was Wordsworth, some of whose poems he had recently read. O to be in the neighbourhood of that man, to see the house in which he dwelt, the scenes amid which he moved; perhaps to catch a glimpse of himself! Alive, however, to the absurdity of any such approach to Wordsworth in the character of a runaway schoolboy, and also to the duty of some communication first of all with his mother, he had determined to run the risks involved in the latter course. As his mother had by this time got tired of Bath, and transferred herself to a house in Chester, called the Priory, the communication was not difficult. Two days of walking carried him over the forty miles that separated Manchester from Chester; and, after some hovering about the house, of which he gives a whimsical account, the meeting took place. His mother, with her notions and habits of decorum, looked upon the occurrence, he says, " much as she would have done upon the opening of the seventh seal in the Revelations ;" but it chanced that another relative was at hand who took a lighter view of the affair. This

was his uncle, Colonel Thomas Penson, his mother's only
surviving brother, home from India on a three-years' furlough, and quartered for the time, with his horses and
Bengalee servants, at the Priory.  Colonel Penson, a
kindly man of the world, saw nothing unnatural in the
desire of a youth to elope from the tedium of school ; and,
by his advice, it was arranged that De Quincey, if he did
not choose to remain at the Priory, should have a guinea
a week allowed him for a while, with liberty to wander
about and enjoy himself on that basis.

From July to November 1802 we see him wandering
about North Wales, from town to town, from village to
village, from country-inn to country-inn, having various
little adventures and picking up random new acquaintances
by the way, all the while making his guinea a week go as
far as it could, and hitting on ingenious devices for that
end.  The chief was that of alternating, according to
whim and weather, between the more expensive style of
living, at the rate of about half-a-guinea a day, necessary
if he went to the better inns, and the incredibly cheap
living then possible in Wales if one lodged in the cottages
of the hospitable and unsophisticated Welsh peasantry, or
snatched a meal somewhere in a long walk and bivouacked
through the night among ferns and furze.  It was, he
says, a most pleasant existence, an existence of breezy
freedom, with perpetual delight from the mountain
scenery, the sylvan nooks, the rushing brooks, the picturesque evening groups of the villagers gathered round
their harpers.  But the sting of some unsatisfied craving,
the fatal longing in his nature to break away from the
customary and respectable and to dare the forbidden and
indefinite, carried him suddenly out of those Welsh
solitudes.  He would give up his guinea a week, cut that

remaining bond between him and his mother and guardians, and bury himself in the world of London. There he would find books and society; there he would find he knew not what; there he would find at least,—so he had heard,—Jew money-lenders, who might be willing to advance him 200*l.* on his expectations.

It was late in November 1802 when, having borrowed twelve guineas from two lawyer friends in Oswestry, De Quincey, after eight-and-twenty hours on the coach from Shrewsbury, was deposited in the streets of London. Here what months he passed, what months of wild, haggard, Bohemian roaming and staggering from worse to worse! He had lost no time in applying to a Jew money-lender, named Dell; but Dell was never himself to be seen in such cases, and the negotiation had to be with Dell's devil or legal factotum. This was a low attorney, called Brunell, who had for his place of business a house in Greek Street, Soho, at the corner of Soho Square, with precautionary chains on the doors, and loopholes through which those who knocked could be surveyed before they were admitted. As we read the description of this house in Greek Street, with all its rooms unoccupied and unfurnished, save Mr. Brunell's own sanctum, and some den for his athletic clerk, Pyment, and of Mr. Brunell's arrivals in it every morning from no one knew where, and his disappearances in the evening, when his sanctum was carefully locked and the empty house was left in the sole keeping of a poor little wretch of a girl, ten years of age, who slept on straw as near as she could to the street-door, we feel as if we were in the midst of a novel by Dickens. With Brunell himself De Quincey became very familiar by frequent visits, and found him, disreputable though he was, a very kindly person, and with a wonderful passion for literature and knowledge, the survival from some happier time when he had hopes of another career than that of a devil for money-lenders. But Brunell could do nothing himself in the matter of the advance, for there was the invisible Dell in the background. The policy of Dell, in such cases, was that of delay,—delay for the necessary investigations, for whetting the appetite of the applicant, and for exacting charges for papers, stamps, and one knows not what. Thus the lad, though living as parsimoniously as he could in lodgings, was brought to his last guinea, and it was an act of charity when Brunell consented to let him use the house in Greek Street as his sleeping asylum at nights. There, sharing a floor in the void tenement with the little wretch of a servant-girl, to whom his advent was a godsend, as a deliverance from her terrors of loneliness, he did sleep, night after night, for some indefinite period, glad to pick up stray crusts in the morning from Brunell's breakfast-table. But, his presence in the house during the day being undesirable, he had to be off every morning, to " sit in the parks or elsewhere," or prowl about the streets as he chose. And what streets he thus came to know, and what eternal circuits among the same streets! Regent Street then was not; and his main range was the great thoroughfare of Oxford Street, with the streets to the north of it as far as the New Road, and the maze of streets on the other or southern side as far as the line of Coventry Street and Piccadilly. Within those bounds he was a peripatetic through days of which he kept no reckoning, and often late at nights, till the watchmen began to recognise his figure, and would sometimes rouse him roughly as he sat on door-steps. As was natural, he became acquainted with other peripatetics, the " street-walkers " in another sense. With this class of unfortunates, and with not a few individuals among them, he tells us, his relations were intimate enough, though all in perfect innocence. One in chief he could never forget. Oh ! that Ann of Oxford Street, the poor girl of sixteen, whose simple and sad history he had come to know, whose goodness of heart shone out even in her degradation, with whom it had become his daily habit to go about by appointment, and who had once saved his life, when he had fainted from exhaustion, by running for wine and stimulants and fetching them for him out of her own scanty money !

A favourable impression had been at last produced on Dell by proofs of De Quincey's former intimacy with Lord Altamont and the Marquis of Sligo. If Mr. De Quincey could fortify his own mere personal security by getting Lord Altamont to be his co-security, Mr. Dell would not mind lending him 200*l.* or even 300*l.* A casual encounter with an old family friend in Albemarle Street having at the same time provided De Quincey with a little ready cash, he bade Ann farewell for a day or two, and took the coach for Eton to broach the matter to Lord Altamont. Unfortunately his lordship had just left Eton for Cambridge ; and all that De Quincey could effect was a provisional arrangement with another young nobleman at Eton, which he thought might answer Mr. Dell's purpose. When he returned to London, Ann was gone ! He never saw her or heard of her more. All his life afterwards that girl was to be in his thoughts. Ah ! poor Ann of Oxford Street, what had become of her ? Had she gone into some ruffianly keeping and might she be still alive ; or had that cough which he had observed in her done its merciful work, and was her young frame at rest, though but in a pauper's grave, in some dank corner of a London churchyard ?

Is all this true, or was De Quincey romancing? He was himself aware that there might be some such suspicion; and, when, immediately after the first publication of his *Confessions*, some of his critics were taking them for ingenious fiction, he was very serious in his efforts to undeceive them. He had not told the *whole* truth about his London vagrancy, he said, because that was impossible, but he had told nothing but the truth. Such an assurance ought itself to count for something; but there is more. In early private letters of De Quincey, published by Mr. Page, we have the means of checking portions of his subsequent autobiographical writings; and, as in all cases where this check can be applied the correspondence between the original memorials and the later narrative is strikingly exact, a slight occasional haziness of date excepted, the rest of the narrative is entitled to the benefit of the fact. In short, though there may be a little mingling of the *Dichtung* with the *Wahrheit*, De Quincey's account of his days of London wretchedness may be accepted as authentic. And why not? True, it could only have been a most odd, unpractical, little creature that could have got himself into such conditions, or that, once in them, could not have extricated himself. But are there not such queer young eccentrics in the world even now, creatures of cleverness touched with some craze or peculiarity which makes them a puzzle to their friends, and which, while incapacitating them for the most obvious acts of reasonableness natural to ordinary people, leads them sometimes to acts at which ordinary people stare? That eccentricity of De Quincey which was to be a life-long characteristic, and even that form of eccentricity which was to be peculiarly his in after-life,— a constant shy timorousness, a perpetual looking backward over his shoulder for some terrible danger that he had

D

escaped, but that was still dogging him,—seems to have
been first developed in those days of his strange London
experiences in his eighteenth year. When Carlyle knew
him long afterwards, and when his small stature, boyish
face, gentle demeanour, and beautiful silvery talk, were the
most obvious things about him to first observation, something more, Carlyle thought, was physiognomically discernible. "*Eccovi !* look at him : this child has been in
Hell."

The proposed substitute for Lord Altamont's guarantee
of co-security not being satisfactory to Mr. Dell, De Quincey
was at the extreme of despair, when, by some unexplained
concatenation of circumstances, he was discovered and
reclaimed by his friends. He went back to Chester, to
reside for some time with his mother in the Priory. His
Indian uncle was still there, and it was some tetchy but
well-intentioned remark of this good gentleman in a
moment of argument that induced De Quincey to close
with a shabby offer made by his guardians, to the effect
that he might go to the University if he liked, but should
not have a farthing more than 100*l.* a year. On this
allowance, in the autumn of 1803, as nearly as the date
can be guessed, he went to Worcester College, Oxford.

## CHAPTER IV.

OF De Quincey's Oxford life very little is known. There is a casual hint from himself that he had made a mistake in his choice of a college. Had he gone to Brasenose, as would have happened if he had remained for the necessary time at Manchester Grammar School, he would have had a smooth and properly arranged introduction to the academic life, whereas in Worcester College he was an isolated stranger, left to shift for himself. All that the head of the college, Dr. Cotton, could afterwards remember of him was summed up in a few sentences. "During the " period of his residence," says Dr. Cotton, "he was " generally known as a quiet and studious man. He did " not frequent wine parties, though he did not abstain " from wine ; and he devoted himself principally to the " society of a German, named Schwartzburg, who is said " to have taught him Hebrew. He was remarkable even " in those days for his rare conversational powers, and for " his extraordinary stock of information upon every subject " that was started." Altogether, though he had some acquaintances in different colleges, and was known among them as a very uncommon person, he seems rather to

have crept through the University quietly than to have
made any stir in it, keeping much by himself, and reading
prodigiously in lines of his own.   This recluseness was
not owing to the extreme necessity of economy which his
guardians had tried to impose upon him when they fixed
his allowance at only 100*l.* a year.   That had been evaded,
he tells us, by the relenting of his Jewish friend in
London, who did at last advance him the sum for which
there had been so much negotiation.   He could thus
afford himself all that was needed to make Oxford student-
ship fairly comfortable, including books, a run to London
now and then, and a visit, in vacation-time, to friends in
Liverpool or elsewhere.

The lessons from the German Schwartzburg were of
some consequence.   They were not in Hebrew merely.
Though he had received some general notions of German
Literature, and especially some tempting information about
Jean Paul Richter, Hippel, Hamann, and other little-
known German writers, from an accomplished young
German, named De Haren, with whom he had formed a
friendship in his Welsh wanderings, it was at Oxford, and
under Schwartzburg, that he first set himself seriously
to the study of German.   The German Philosophy, as
well as the German Literature, attracted him thenceforward.

Of even greater importance was the systematic attention
he now began to bestow on English Literature.   Though
from his childhood his sensibilities had been powerfully
affected by "the greatness of our own literature," and though
his readings in English poets and prose-writers had been
extensive and varied, it was at Oxford that he first felt
the necessity of organizing his knowledge of English
Literature, and regarding it no longer as a mere splendid

phenomenon or sky of so many hundreds of scattered
stars of different degrees of brilliancy, but as a vast and
vital whole that could be grasped in a History. Thenceforward, while Chaucer, Spenser, Shakespeare, Bacon,
Milton, Sir Thomas Browne, Jeremy Taylor, and others of
his favourites among the older writers, were dearer and
more distinct to him than ever individually, he could
contemplate that great flow of the national thought through
successive centuries, which, though it seemed to eddy
round those individualities as so many independent and
inserted marvels, had really caused them and stationed
them where they were, and which, after its farther, and
in his eyes less interesting, course through the eighteenth
century, was now again becoming glorious in Wordsworth
and his disciples. It was on this last portion of the long
history of English Literature, the portion contemporary
with himself, that De Quincey fastened his regard with the
enthusiasm of a personal concern. He had by this time
put himself in correspondence with Wordsworth, express-
ing his admiration and indebtedness, and had received at
least two letters of reply, intimating that the poet was not
indifferent to the recognition of such a hopeful young
admirer, and would be glad to see him at a convenient
opportunity. More recently, he had been making inquiries
after Coleridge, whom he had known first by his *Ancient
Mariner*, published with Wordsworth's *Lyrical Ballads*
in 1798, but to whom he was now drawn also by interest
in his prose-writings. As De Quincey had already concluded with himself that it would never be in the element
of verse that his own genius could accomplish anything
considerable in literature, if he should ever accomplish
anything at all, the fact that Coleridge was a prose writer
and philosopher, as well as a poet, seems to have whetted

the desire for an immediate meeting with him, if only in preparation for the more formidable and less accessible Wordsworth. He was therefore much disappointed at finding, in 1805, that Coleridge had left the Lakes, and had gone to Malta as Secretary to Sir Alexander Ball, the Governor of that island.

One other fact of De Quincey's days of Oxford student-ship is expressly recorded by himself. It was then that he first began to take opium. His first experience of the drug was on a dull rainy Sunday in the spring or autumn of 1804, when, being on one of his visits to London, and having suffered for a week or two from neuralgia, he took the advice of a friend and purchased a phial of the tinc-ture of opium at a druggist's shop in Oxford Street, near " the stately Pantheon." The effect, when he took the first dose in his lodgings, was divine ; and from that moment De Quincey was an experimenter in opium,— never without a supply of the drug beside him in one or other of its forms, whether in the solid cakes or sticks of the dried substance, as imported from Turkey, Egypt, Persia, or India, or in the prepared red-brown liquid known as laudanum. Nay more, from that moment he was the apologist for opium, skilled, or fancying himself skilled, in all its effects, and distinguishing its negative effects in the mere relief of pain from its positive effects as an intellectual stimulant and exhilarant. He suggests, indeed, that, in continuing the use of the drug after its first service to him in an attack of neuralgia, he had hit by blind instinct on the specific for the pulmonary con-sumption to which he was liable by inheritance from his father. The reports of medical authorities, from an in-vestigation of all the evidence, are rather to the effect that the constitutional disease from which he suffered was a

slow or intermittent ulceration of the stomach, brought on
perhaps by bad and insufficient food during his time of
vagrancy in Wales and London, and that his perseverance
in the use of opium was due originally to his accidental
experience of its effects in allaying those " gnawing pains
in the stomach " of which, from that time of his vagrancy,
he complained always or periodically. Enough of a
disagreeable subject. What concerns us at present is that
De Quincey avers most solemnly that, though he took
opium at Oxford from 1804 onwards, it was still in such
moderation that he could have broken off the habit. He
was not yet, nor for some years to come, a slave to opium
but confined himself to a carefully præcalculated opium-
debauch, as he calls it, about once in three weeks. The
probability is that the indulgence added to his queerness
among the Oxonians, his liking for solitary reverie, and his
carelessness of academic routine and distinction.

De Quincey, it seems, did go up for his written exami-
nation for the degree of B.A. The fact is attested by
one of his old schoolfellows at Winkfield, who had gone
to Lincoln College while De Quincey was in residence in
Worcester College. Dr. Goodenough of Christ Church,
says this authority, was wonderfully struck with De
Quincey's performance, and told the Worcester College
people that they had sent up the cleverest man he had
ever encountered, and that, if he did as well in his *vivâ
voce* as he had done on paper, he would carry all before
him. But De Quincey, in a fit of shyness, or having taken
some offence, never presented himself for his *vivâ voce*,
remained without his degree, and indeed disappeared from
Oxford for some time. The date is not given, but it seems
to have been in 1807. His name remained on the books
of his college till 1810 ; but, as we have his own distinct

statement that his time of residence was from 1803 to
1808, we have to suppose only a year of effective connexion with the University after 1807, and that broken
by absences. He liked to be in London, where he now
counted Charles Lamb in the number of his acquaintances,
and where he delighted in going to the Opera to hear
Grassini sing, and in rambling among the markets on Saturday nights ; and he had entered himself, or was about to
enter himself, as a member of the Middle Temple, with
a view to eating his terms for the Bar. His mother
meanwhile having shifted her domicile from Chester to
a house and estate called Westhay, in Somersetshire, about
twelve miles from Bristol, which had been purchased for
her by her Indian brother at a cost of 12,000*l.*, there were
visits also to that part of the West of England, with
renewed confabulations with Hannah More and her set.
What is of especial importance in De Quincey's biography,
however, at this time of the close of his residence at
Oxford, is that he is found then indubitably in possession
of a good deal of money. How this had come about we
are not informed ; but, as he had attained his majority in
1806, we are to fancy either that he had then been put
at comparative ease by becoming master of his own funds,
or that there had been some new and enlarged transaction
with the Jews, converting the whole futurity of those
funds into a present capital. As De Quincey speaks of
his transactions with the Jews as pretty continuous, or as
repeated from time to time, in his earlier life, the latter
supposition is likely enough.

The improvement of De Quincey's pecuniary circumstances in and from the year 1807 connects itself more
particularly with one interesting absence of his from Oxford
in the latter half of that year. Having gone into Somerset-

shire in the course of the summer, and having heard that
Coleridge had returned from abroad, and was then quartered
among friends at Nether Stowey in that county, he went
in search of the great man. He did not find him at
Nether Stowey, but came upon him in the town of Bridge-
water, where he was staying, with his wife, and his three
young children, Hartley, Derwent, and Sara, in the house
of a certain family of Chubbs, well-to-do descendants of
Chubb the Deist. It was a memorable meeting. The
"noticeable man with large grey eyes," now not more
than thirty-five years of age, but, as De Quincey observed,
with flabby and unhealthy white cheeks and confused and
abstracted gait, received his young visitor very courteously,
and had several conversations with him, by himself and
in company. Though the elder opium-eater and the
younger opium-eater were thus together, no confidences
were exchanged on that subject, save that once, when
laudanum was casually mentioned by De Quincey, it was
with an emphasis of horror that Coleridge warned him to
have nothing to do with that drug. The talk, or rather
Coleridge's monologue, was on all things and sundry, and
De Quincey was amazed, even beyond expectation, by its
range and gorgeousness. His veneration for Coleridge
became a kind of filial affection ; and, when, a few weeks
after, Coleridge went with his family to Bristol and their
acquaintance was renewed there, it was with delight that
De Quincey found he could do the sage a slight piece of
service. Mrs. Coleridge and the children were bound for
the Lakes, to be domiciled, as before, with Southey at Greta
Hall, Keswick ; but, as Coleridge was arranging for a course
of lectures on Poetry and the Fine Arts, to be delivered
at the Royal Institution in Albemarle Street, London, he
could not accompany them. De Quincey offered to be

their escort ; and in October 1807 the party set out from
Bristol by post-chaise.   Travelling by stages, and with
some little stay at Liverpool, they reached the Lake
Country by a route which required them to take Wordsworth's cottage at Grasmere as their resting-place before
going on to Southey's at Keswick.  Twice had De Quincey
been on the verge of this poetic paradise before, but both
times he had retreated with a nervous shrinking at the
last moment from the idea of presenting himself to
Wordsworth.   Now, however, in his character of convoy
to Mrs. Coleridge, rather than in that of Wordsworth's
occasional correspondent in past years, he did behold the
epoch-making man, received a grasp of welcome from his
hand at his own door, and became his temporary guest.
For two days he was in the cottage, along with Mrs.
Coleridge and her children, happy in the society of Wordsworth, his wife, and his sister Dorothy, and making his
observations of the three ; and on the third day there
began that excursion of all the seniors of the party over
the hills in a cart, which, while it deposited Mrs. Coleridge
at her destination in Southey's house, gave De Quincey
his first introduction also to that other famous Lakist.
All this was in November 1807 ; before the end of which
month De Quincey was back in Bristol, to hear of the
completion of another piece of kindness he had been
meditating for Coleridge.   The profound dejection of
Coleridge, the state of "cheerless despondency" into
which he had fallen, and out of which his splendid talks
were evidently but leaps and refuges of despair, had struck
his young friend ; and, having ascertained by inquiries
that the main immediate cause was hopeless distress in
money-matters, De Quincey had been in private communication with Cottle, the Bristol bookseller, on the subject.

He wanted to give Coleridge 500*l.*, a sum which all
Cottle's representations, with questions whether he was
serious, whether he could afford it, whether he was of age,
&c., could not persuade him to reduce below 300*l.* That
sum Coleridge did accept, having been told nothing more
by Cottle at the time than that " a young man of fortune
who admired his talents " wanted to make him a present.
Coleridge's formal receipt for the money, which the bookseller thought it right to take for his own exoneration, is
dated November 12, 1807.

Though De Quincey includes the year 1808 in the time
of his Oxford residence, the records show him to have
been much in London through parts of that year. Coleridge was one of his attractions. He heard some of the
sage's lectures at the Royal Institution, and regretted that,
from Coleridge's own carelessness in preparation and the
wretched state of his health, they were so nearly a break-
down ; he saw much of Coleridge in his uncomfortable
temporary chambers in the office of the *Courier* newspaper
in the Strand ; and in his calls on Coleridge at these chambers he met Sir Humphry Davy, Godwin, and other new
faces. Later in the year he is found still, or again, in
London, in lodgings in Titchfield Street and Northumber-
land Street, Marylebone, eating his terms, one has to
suppose, and seeing Lamb and Hazlitt, and sauntering at
nights among the markets, and not failing at the opera for
many nights in succession. In November of the same
year he paid a second visit to Wordsworth at the Lakes ;
and he remained there till February 1809, when he
returned to London. Wordsworth, at the time of this
second visit of De Quincey, had been busy with that
series of political letters in the *Courier* newspaper which
he converted into more complete form in his pamphlet,

published May 1809, *Concerning the Relations of Great
Britain, Spain, and Portugal, as affected by the Conven-
tion of Cintra.* It was De Quincey, after his return to
London, who saw this pamphlet through the press, adding
an appendix of notes, which Wordsworth described as
"done in a masterly manner." The service was gratefully
acknowledged also by Wordsworth's sister, Dorothy. A
letter of hers is extant in which she thanks De Quincey
warmly for having saved her brother so much anxiety,
says he had been a treasure to them both, and hopes
that he may soon be at Grasmere to refresh himself
after the troubles of his task.

Dorothy Wordsworth's hope in this letter points to an
arrangement of some importance that had been come to
between De Quincey and the Wordsworths. This was
that De Quincey should leave London, Oxford, and all
his other troublesome entanglements in the south, and
should come to reside permanently at the Lakes, as the
tenant of the very cottage in which Wordsworth had lived
from 1799 to 1807, but which he had recently quitted
for the somewhat larger house, called Allan Bank, about a
mile distant. Through the latter months of 1809 the talk
among the inhabitants of the quiet valley of Grasmere
was of the young gentleman who was coming to live
among them in Mr. Wordsworth's old cottage, and of
Miss Wordsworth's careful activity in ordering carpets
and other furnishings, and getting the cottage ready for
his arrival.

# CHAPTER V.

In November 1809, De Quincey, at the age of twenty-four, took possession of his pretty cottage at Town-end, Grasmere, and became one of the so-called Lakists. For seven and twenty years this cottage was to be in his tenancy, and for more than twenty of these it was to be his headquarters and nominal home, the place where he resided constantly when he was at rest, or to which he always returned from any of his frequent divagations.

Strange that a district of England which had been sleeping unknown in its native beauties and grandeurs from time immemorial, over whose mountains the snow had come and gone silently for a thousand winters, and whose valleys had laughed again in equal privacy into shower and sunshine through the thousand alternating summers, should have been suddenly evoked into celebrity by the genius of one man. But so it had happened. Wordsworth was making the Lake District, and the call had gone forth to come and behold it. Ho! all ye that are tourists and in quest of the picturesque, try this district in the proper season; all ye that have made a little money, and desire to settle somewhere, in peace and

meditative comfort, for the rest of your lives, examine
these valleys and the skirts of these lakes for the suitable
spots; all ye that are sons of the muses in the higher
sense, not tied by hard necessity to the vicinity of a
printing-press, in London, or Edinburgh, or any other city,
but at liberty to select an abode where you may possess
your souls in quiet and combine high thinking with plain
living,—Mr. Wordsworth uses and recommends no beve-
rages stronger than milk or tea; but stronger may be imported if indispensable, and there are inns on the roads,—
come and have cottages here, and spend hours every day
in the open air, communing with Nature herself, as she
is to be found, pure and unsophisticated, in Cumberland
and Westmoreland scenery! By the year 1809 the response had been considerable. Tourists had been becoming numerous enough to suggest to Wordsworth the
rudiments of what afterwards took form as his *Guide to
the Lakes ;* new residents from among the class of retired
business-men were appearing by degrees; and, though
fewer sons of the muses were in circumstances to accept
the invitation than might have liked to do so, a sprinkling
of such was to be counted.

Wordsworth himself, now in his fortieth year, and
settled at Grasmere since 1799, had just, as we have seen,
migrated from his previous cottage to Allan Bank, only
a mile distant, which was to be his residence till the spring
of 1811, when he transferred himself to Grasmere Par-
sonage, there to remain till 1813, when he removed to his
final and most famous residence of Rydal Mount. Southey,
the industrious Southey, four years younger than Wordsworth, had been established for some years at Greta Hall,
Keswick, in the Cumberland portion of the Lake District,
and at least thirteen miles from Wordsworth. It was a

convenient distance between two men whose mutual respect
obliged them to occasional intercourse, but whose styles of
genius and habits of literary work were so different as
to cause some degree of mutual repulsion.   Coleridge,
Southey's brother-in-law, who had been a Lakist in previous years, and quartered for some time, with his family,
in Southey's house, had, as we have seen, broken away
from the Lakes for a while, gone abroad, gone to
Somersetshire, but again gravitated to the mill-horse
round of London.   Having sent his wife and children
back to Southey's, however, he had at length followed
them himself, to try the Lakes once more ; and, from late
in 1809 to the middle of 1810, Coleridge was to be again
a denizen of the district, moving between Southey's at
Keswick and Wordsworth's at Grasmere, but on the whole
preferring to be with Wordsworth.   Here, through that
time, he was to be engaged in bringing out his periodical
called *The Friend*, which was printed at Penrith, and the
bad management of which was to bring the whole concern to bankruptcy in the twenty-ninth number.   Three
other literary notabilities of the Lake District, at the time
of De Quincey's advent there, deserve especial mention.
One was Dr. Richard Watson, Bishop of Llandaff, now
seventy-two years of age, but with seven years of life still
before him, living at his mansion of Calgarth Park, on Windermere, eight miles south from Grasmere, and altogether
the leading personage in the society of the region, from
his ecclesiastical rank and great wealth, his hospitality
and conversational ability, and the recollection of his
extraordinary series of publications.   A much humbler
man, but loved beyond expression by all his intimate
friends, was Charles Lloyd, living at Brathay, about half-
way between Calgarth and Grasmere, originally a Quaker,

but now a kind of Lakist Rousseau, revealing philosophic powers that had not been guessed from his published poems. The time was yet some years distant when this fine intellect, overclouded by a growing lunacy, was to be withdrawn from Brathay to die abroad. Finally, a recent comer into the Lake District, proprietor since 1807 of Elleray, also on Windermere, about a mile from Calgarth, was a young Scoto-Oxonian of whom the world was to hear more than of either Bishop Watson or Charles Lloyd. This was John Wilson, afterwards known as Professor Wilson and "Christopher North." He was almost exactly of De Quincey's own age, or but three months older ; but what a contrast between them physically,—De Quincey one of the smallest and feeblest-looking of mortals, hardly more than five feet high, while Wilson was one of the most magnificent young athletes that ever attracted men's or women's eyes in street or on heather. His stature close on six feet, his frame proportioned into the very ideal of a Hercules-Apollo of the Scandinavian or yellow-haired type, masking immensity of strength under the litheness of a leopard, he carried also one of the noblest and most poetic of heads ever set on beautifully square human shoulders. Then, what a reputation he had brought with him from Oxford, where, strangely enough, he had been a gentleman-commoner of Magdalen College all the time of De Quincey's residence in the University, though they had never then met ! While De Quincey had been creeping through the University, a bookish opium-eating recluse, Wilson had been the most observed man of all the colleges, not more for his magnificent physique and his unapproachable applications of it in pugilistic matches, leaping matches, and all other kinds of University sports, than for his universal sociability, exuberance of humour, easy triumphs in the classics and whatever else he cared to compete in, and promises of some unusual form of literary effulgence not yet distinctly featured. With this kind of reputation preceding him from Oxford, it was as if he had bounded into the Lake District, rather than merely settled in it ; and already the splendid young Mr. Wilson of Elleray, to whom his father, a Paisley manufacturer, had left a clear fortune of 50,000*l.*, was known not only to all his neighbours that were likely to think of that matter, but also to every boatman, every innkeeper, every crack wrestler or boxer, every band of gipsies or other vagrants, over the whole region.

In this mere enumeration there is already implied a good deal of De Quincey's life through the six or seven years at present under notice. The mile of road from his own cottage to Wordsworth's house of Allan Bank was his familiar walk morning and evening from the first, for the sake of Wordsworth's society, and also of Coleridge's, so long as Coleridge, busy in bringing out his *Friend,* remained Wordsworth's guest. As many as 500 books at a time from the very considerable library which De Quincey had in his cottage, a large portion of it consisting of German books, would, he tells us, be in Wordsworth's house in those days for Coleridge's use,— Wordsworth's own library being the most wretched thing that ever went by that name, a mere litter of tattered odd volumes on a few shelves. The distance from Southey, whose library was the chief distinction of his house, prevented such frequent intercourse with him as with the Wordsworths ; nor was De Quincey ever bound to Southey by any very close intimacy. He did occasionally visit at Greta Hall, however, and was able, " in a

E

qualified sense," to call Southey his friend; and we find Southey, in a letter to a correspondent in 1810, making mention of De Quincey in rather memorable terms. "De Quincey," he says, 'is a singular man, but better informed than any person almost that I ever met at his age." That De Quincey was among the numerous visitors of the great Bishop Watson at Calgarth Park, and thus came to know that celebrity personally, is no mere guess. "This dignitary," he tells us, "I knew myself as much as I wished to know him: he *was* interesting; yet also *not* interesting;" and he goes on to sketch for us his portrait of the somewhat pompous and worldly, yet kindly, jovial, candid, and strong-headed septuagenarian, whom, pluralist and sinecurist though he had been all his life, and all but avowedly at his own table a Socinian and free-thinker, the Whigs had wished to make Archbishop of York. At Brathay De Quincey was a constant visitor, sometimes in solitary conversation for hours with the philosophic Charles Lloyd himself, sometimes at one of Lloyd's well-attended dinner parties, sometimes looking on at one of those evening parties of young people that Lloyd liked to see gathered at his house. It had been at one of these evening parties at Lloyd's, apparently in the year 1808, that De Quincey had first seen Wilson,—dancing radiantly and indefatigably, and chiefly with a Miss Jane Penny, "the leading belle of the Lake Country;" but it was in Wordsworth's house that the first formal introduction took place. It was Wordsworth himself, when De Quincey entered his room one morning and found a stranger with him, that pronounced the words of introduction, "*Mr. Wilson of Elleray*," in his usual deep tones. From the time of this introduction the two were fast friends, some unusually strong elective affinity attaching the magnificent master of Elleray to his puny neighbour. There was talk between them of a tour together to Spain, the Mediterranean, and the East; and, though that came to nothing, they contrived to be together as much as possible, whenever Wilson was at Elleray, and not, as happened pretty often, away in Edinburgh on the business of his nominal preparation for the Scottish Bar. It must have been a sight to see the two together in one of Wilson's fishing expeditions among the Lakes, or in their joint rambles over the hills, the little De Quincey trudging side by side with his majestic comrade. But De Quincey was a capital walker, never satisfied without his ten or fifteen miles daily in the open air. Even in that matter, therefore, he and Wilson were well enough matched; while it may be doubted whether in the subtle, scholarly, whimsical, and deeply reasoned bits of brain-product which the smaller man gave to the larger in the course of their walks, in exchange for the laughs and wild immethodic chaunts which prophesied the future Christopher, the larger man may not have had the better bargain. When Wilson was not at Elleray, or even when he was there, De Quincey delighted much in long, aimless walks by himself, especially nocturnal walks.

More and more, it seems, after 1810, when Coleridge took his final departure from the Lakes, there had been a gradual waning of the friendship between De Quincey and Wordsworth. They were still much together; Wordsworth still consulted De Quincey about his poems, or lines in his poems; and De Quincey's admiration of the hero in his poetic character remained unabated. But, whether because Wordsworth, in his self-absorption, found De Quincey's companionship unnecessary, or because De Quincey felt his nerves jarred by Wordsworth's habitual austerity and masculine hardness, certain it is that there came at length to be some degree of mutual alienation. This was recompensed in part by the fidelity of Dorothy Wordsworth's liking for De Quincey and by the growing attachment to him of Wordsworth's children. The Wordsworth children were never tired of talking of " Kinsey," and the presents he brought them. " Kinsey! Kinsey! what a' bring Katy from London?" were the parting words of one of them, his favourite little Kate Wordsworth, as he was going away for a while. He remembered the words and quoted them in a letter which he wrote to Dorothy Wordsworth on hearing of the young thing's death in his absence, June 4, 1812. His grief over the death of this child passed all that is common in that kind of experience.

Only a part of the life of a man, even at the Lakes, can consist in walks and talks out-of-doors with friends, or in visits to the houses of neighbours. Much of it, all the best of it, must consist in what he does by himself within the four walls that enclose him when he is not dependent on others. Have we any glimpse of De Quincey and his occupations in his solitary bachelorhood in his pretty, rose-embowered, cottage at Grasmere? We have ; and it ought to be quoted. It is the passage where, overleaping the interval from his Oxford life, he presents himself as he was in 1812, two hundred and fifty miles away from Oxford, and buried among mountains:—

And what am I doing amongst the mountains? Taking opium. Yes; but what else? Why, reader, in 1812, the year we are now arrived at, as well as for some years previous, I have been chiefly studying German metaphysics, or the writings of Kant, Fichte, Schelling, &c. And how, and in what manner

do I live? in short, what class or description of men do I
belong to? I am at this period,—viz., in 1812,—living in a
cottage; and with a single female servant (*honi soit qui mal y
pense*), who, amongst my neighbours, passes by the name of
my "housekeeper." And, as a scholar and a man of learned
education, I may presume to class myself as an unworthy
member of that indefinite body called *gentlemen*. Partly on
the ground I have assigned,—partly because, from having
no visible calling or business, it is rightly judged that I
must be living on my private fortune,—I am so classed by
my neighbours; and, by the courtesy of modern England,
I am usually addressed on letters, &c., *Esquire*. . . . Am I
married? Not yet. And I still take opium? On Saturday nights. And, perhaps, have taken it unblushingly ever
since "the rainy Sunday," and "the stately Pantheon," and
"the beatific druggist" of 1804? Even so. And how do I
find my health after all this opium-eating? in short, how do I
do? Why, pretty well, I thank you, reader. In fact, if I dared
to say the real and simple truth (though, in order to satisfy the
theories of some medical men, I ought to be ill), I was never
better in my life than in the spring of 1812; and I hope sin-
cerely that the quantity of claret, port, or "London particular
Madeira," which, in all probability, you, good reader, have
taken, and design to take, for every term of eight years during
your natural life, may as little disorder your health as mine was
disordered by all the opium I had taken (though in quantity
such that I might well have bathed and swum in it) for the
eight years between 1804 and 1812.

Translated into stricter biographical language, this
means, in the first place, that De Quincey had been a
hard student during his residence at the Lakes, burning
the midnight oil a good deal over his books of all sorts,
but especially over the later German transcendentalists.
Nothing is said of that other exercise which is the sole
salvation of any man situated as De Quincey was, and
without which reading and reverie are but an Epicurean
waste of spirit,—actual *production* of some kind or other,

by a wide-awake exertion of one's own faculties, out of the
stuff of one's readings and reveries. We may, however,
if we choose, suppose piles of papers on his table, if only
in the form of abstracts of the books read, and comments
and criticisms on them for his own edification. Of this
we are less certain than of the other fact of which the
extract assures us. He had brought the habit of opium-
taking to the Lakes with him; and an indispensable
article on his table, on one night of the week at least,
when he was seated by himself, and the shutters were
shut, and the candles lit, and the fire burning brightly,
was the opium decanter !

De Quincey's intimations on this subject are perfectly
plain. Through the eight years preceding 1812 he had,
he says, persisted uninterruptedly in the use of opium,
with a gradual increase both in the frequency of his doses
and of the quantity of each, but still,—so he could flatter
himself,—with no signs of permanent injury. But, within
a year, he goes on to say, the case was altered. The year
1813, he intimates, was a fatal one in his history. There
had been some calamity of a private kind, causing him
great distress. What it was he does not say; but it seems
to have been some serious catastrophe in his pecuniary
affairs. This may be inferred from a letter to him from
his uncle, Colonel Penson, sent from Futtygur in India,
and dated 16th July, 1813. "I have heard that your
" affairs are not prosperous," the letter begins, " though
" of the nature or extent of your misfortunes I have no
" information. Yet, as it has pleased God to bless me
" beyond either hope or expectation since I left England,
" I feel that in requesting your acceptance of the enclosed
" I am not violating," &c. What the good uncle enclosed
was a handsome draft for his nephew's help. It may

have been to the same unfortunate crisis in De Quincey's affairs that there had been reference in a note sent him by Wordsworth some months before, when he was away on one of his rambles from Grasmere. The main purpose was to inform him of the death of another of Words-worth's children, little Tommy, who had been a pet of De Quincey's; but the note ends, "Most tenderly and lovingly, with heavy sorrow for you, my dear friend, I remain yours, W. WORDSWORTH." Whether the calamity was of the kind here suggested or not, it had very important effects on De Quincey's health, and, through them, on his dealings with opium. "I was attacked," he says, " by a most appalling irritation of the stomach, in all re- " spects the same as that which had caused me so much " suffering in youth, and accompanied by a revival of the " old dreams. Now, then, it was,—viz., in the year " 1813,—that I became a regular and confirmed (no " longer an intermitting) opium-eater." He explains what he means by informing us that from this time the use of the drug increased and increased upon him till it reached the monstrous allowance of 320 grains of solid opium, or 8000 drops of laudanum, per day. It may convey a more exact idea if we add that 8000 drops would fill about seven ordinary wine-glasses.

That this exchange of the practice of a periodical or intermittent opium-debauch for the character of a con-firmed and daily opium-eater, was accompanied by some speedy experience of those opium-horrors of which he has left us such vivid descriptions, may be taken for granted. It is to a later period, however, that he refers his full experience of those opium-horrors; and what we should gather from his brief accounts of himself for the year or two immediately following 1813 is rather that he was not

yet in the stage of that most awful experience of the effects
of opium, but simply under an increasing cloud of gloom,
with a torpor of the intellectual faculties. The recorded
incidents of those years are very few, and relate chiefly to
some rambles away from the Lakes. Several times, as we
are told, he was in London ; and every year, it appears,
he was for some time in Somersetshire or elsewhere in the
West of England, visiting his mother and her friends. It
was in one of those visits to Somersetshire, in 1814, and
at Hannah More's house, that he met Mrs. Siddons, then
retiring from the stage in her fifty-ninth year, and was
amused by an animated debate which he heard between
the two ladies on the points of Calvinism, till Hannah
More's ladylike tact changed the subject and wiled Mrs.
Siddons into her charming recollections of Johnson and
Garrick. But a more memorable visit than any to Somersetshire was that which he paid to Edinburgh, for the first
time, in the winter of 1814-15.

Wilson, who had been a married man since 1811, when
the fore-mentioned Miss Jane Penny, the belle of the
Lake District, became his wife, had been coming and
going as before between Edinburgh and Elleray. He had
also published his *Isle of Palms* and other poems ; he was
about to be called to the Edinburgh Bar ; and, being still
in the enjoyment of his large patrimonial fortune, though
very soon to lose it by the misconduct of a relative, he
was now, in his thirtieth year, a shining figure in Edinburgh society. Twice or thrice he had tried to bring De
Quincey with him from the Lakes ; but not till now had
he succeeded. The months of the winter of 1814-15
which De Quincey did spend in Edinburgh were a subject of brilliant recollection long afterwards. Of Scott
and Jeffrey he seems to have seen nothing, or nothing

more than their physiognomies in the streets or the Parliament House; but the group of less-known but rising men that was gathered round Wilson and his brothers, forming the Young Edinburgh of that date, was sufficiently interesting in itself. There was Sir William Hamilton, in his twenty-seventh year, already nominally a Scottish advocate, but really an omnivorous scholar, and, as the world came in time to know, the nearest approach to an Aristotle *redivivus* in the British Logic and Metaphysics of his generation. There was Sir William's younger brother, Thomas Hamilton, known afterwards as the author of *Cyril Thornton*, a novel of considerable merit. There was Scott's friend, William Allan the painter, afterwards Sir William Allan and President of the Royal Scottish Academy. There was a certain Robert Pierce Gillies, of the Scottish Bar, more of an invalid than the rest of the group, but versatile in literature, full of literary gossip, and noted in those days for the "all but princely" style of his hospitalities. Finally, not to mention others then walking the Parliament House as budding barristers, afterwards to be judges or big-wigs of some kind, there was John Gibson Lockhart, yet only in his twenty-first year, and not to be called to the Bar till two years hence, but already beginning to be recognised on the verge of the Young Edinburgh set for his literary promise and his scorpion readiness in sting and caricature. In the circle of these, with Wilson's house as the centre, De Quincey moved during his stay in Edinburgh, welcome among them from the first, and leaving among them no ordinary impression. Mr. R. P. Gillies has commemorated particularly the effects of his conversation. "The talk might be " of ' beeves,' and he could grapple with them, if expected " to do so : but his musical cadences were not in keeping

" with such work, and in a few minutes (not without
" some strictly logical sequence) he would escape at will
" from beeves to butterflies, and thence to the soul's im-
" mortality, to Plato, and Kant, and Schelling, and
" Fichte, to Milton's early years and Shakespeare's Son-
" nets, to Wordsworth and Coleridge, to Homer and
" Æschylus, to St. Thomas of Aquin, St. Basil, and St.
" Chrysostom." As yet, it is to be remembered De
Quincey had not published a line of his own.

For incidents in De Quincey's bachelor life at the
Lakes after his return from Edinburgh we search in vain,
unless we may count among them his famous, but un-
dated, adventure with the Malay. He was sitting in his
room in his cottage one day when he was informed that
there was a strange dark man in the kitchen. Going to
the rescue of the alarmed girl who had admitted the man,
he found him to be a poor Malay tramp, in a turban and
dingy white trousers, whom some accident had brought
into those parts. He had some food and rest; and, at his
departure, De Quincey, who could not understand a word
he said, but guessed that as an Asiatic he might be no
stranger to opium, presented him with some. The Malay,
after looking at the piece given him, "enough to kill
some half-dozen dragoons together with their horses," immediately bolted the whole at one mouthful. De Quincey
felt anxious for some days; but, as he never heard that
a dead Malay had been found on the roads thereabouts,
he became satisfied that no harm had been done.

# CHAPTER VI.

MARRIED LIFE AT THE LAKES : PROSTRATION UNDER OPIUM
PROVINCIAL EDITORSHIP.

1816—1821.

WE have had a picture from De Quincey himself of his
life in his cottage at Grasmere in the year 1812.   Here is
a companion picture, also by himself, of his life in the
same cottage in 1816-17 :—

Let there be a cottage, standing in a valley, eighteen miles
from any town ; no spacious valley, but about two miles long by
three-quarters of a mile in average width,—the benefit of which
provision is that all families resident within its circuit will com-
prise, as it were, one larger household, personally familiar to your
eye, and more or less interesting to your affections.   Let the
mountains be real mountains, between 3000 and 4000 feet
high, and the cottage a real cottage, not (as a witty author has
it) "a cottage with a double coach-house;" let it be, in fact (for
I must abide by the actual scene), a white cottage, embowered
with flowering shrubs, so chosen as to unfold a succession of
flowers upon the walls, and clustering around the windows,
through all the months of spring, summer, and autumn ; beginning, in fact, with May roses, and ending with jasmine.
Let it, however, *not* be spring, nor summer, nor autumn, but
winter in its sternest shape. . . . But here, to save myself the
trouble of too much verbal description, I will introduce a painter,
and give him directions for the rest of the picture.   Painters do
not like white cottages, unless a good deal weather-stained ; but,

as the reader now understands that it is a winter night, his
services will not be required except for the *inside* of the house.—
Paint me, then, a room seventeen feet by twelve, and not more
than seven and a half feet high. This, reader, is somewhat
ambitiously styled, in my family, the drawing-room; but, being
contrived " a double debt to pay," it is also, and more justly,
termed the library; for it happens that books are the only
article of property in which I am richer than my neighbours.
Of these I have about 5000, collected gradually since my
eighteenth year. Therefore, painter, put as many as you can
into this room. Make it populous with books; and, further-
more, paint me a good fire, and furniture plain and modest,
befitting the unpretending cottage of a scholar. And near the
fire paint me a tea-table; and (as it is clear that no creature can
come to see me on such a stormy night) place only two cups
and saucers on the tea-tray; and, if you know how to paint such
a thing, symbolically or otherwise, paint me an eternal tea-
pot,—eternal *a parte ante* and *a parte post;* for I usually
drink tea from eight o'clock at night to four in the morning.
And, as it is very unpleasant to make tea, or to pour it out, for
one's self, paint me a lovely young woman sitting at the table.
Paint her arms like Aurora's, and her smiles like Hebe's; but
no, dear M——! not even in jest let me insinuate that thy
power to illuminate my cottage rests upon a tenure so perishable
as mere personal beauty, or that the witchcraft of angelic smiles
lies within the empire of any earthly pencil. Pass, then, my
good painter, to something more within its power; and the next
article brought forward should naturally be myself,—a picture
of the Opium-eater, with his " little golden receptacle of the
pernicious drug " lying beside him on the table. As to the
opium, I have no objection to see a picture of *that;* you may
paint it, if you choose; but I apprise you that no "little"
receptacle would, even in 1816, answer *my* purpose, who was
at a distance from the "stately Pantheon" and all druggists
(mortal or otherwise). No: you may as well paint the real
receptacle, which was not of gold, but of glass, and as much
like a sublunary wine-decanter as possible. In fact, one day,
by a series of happily conceived experiments, I discovered that

it *was* a decanter. Into this you may put a quart of ruby-coloured laudanum; that, and a book of German metaphysics placed by its side, will sufficiently attest my being in the neighbourhood.

The fair tea-maker of this passage, styled "dear M——," was De Quincey's wife, whom he married in the end of 1816. She was a Margaret Simpson, daughter of a small Westmoreland farmer, living at a place called "The Nab," near De Quincey's cottage, and sometimes confounded now with that cottage by tourists, the rather because De Quincey alternated a good deal between the two after his marriage. At the date of the marriage the bride was eighteen years of age, De Quincey being thirty-one. For a while before the event, and in anticipation of it, De Quincey had, as he tells us, "suddenly and without any considerable effort," reduced his daily allowance of opium from 320 grains or 8000 drops to 40 grains or 1000 drops. The effect had been magical. The "cloud of profoundest melancholy" which had rested on his brain passed away; his mind could think as healthily as ever before; he could read Kant again, or any other hard writer, with clear intelligence. And so for a while after the marriage, till he could count about a year altogether of parenthetic peace and happiness in this portion of his life. "It was a year of brilliant water (to speak after the "manner of jewellers), set, as it were, and insulated, in "the gloomy umbrage of opium." For, as he goes on to inform us, his restriction of himself to the diminished allowance was but temporary; and from some time in 1817, on through 1818, and even into 1819, he was again under the full dominion of the fell agent, rising once more to his 8000 drops *per diem*, or even sometimes to 12,000 drops. This, accordingly, was the time of that most intimate and tremendous experience of the opium-horrors in his own case which he has described in part of his *Confessions*.

His description fully bears out the accepted belief, confirmed so strikingly by the similar case of Coleridge, that one inevitable effect of opium-eating is paralysis of the will. With his intellectual apprehensions of duty as keen as ever, he could propose or execute nothing ; he was as powerless as an infant for any practical effort. Every-thing was neglected or procrastinated ; the domestic eco-nomy, so far as it depended on himself, might have gone to wreck ; letters, however urgent, lay about unanswered. Further, there was a paralysis of that very physical craving which, if gratified, might have furnished so far a counteractive to the opium. While he had always before needed and liked long walks, and while his sole chance now lay in enormous exercise of that kind, he sank into a state of hopeless sedentariness. Add to all this the protracted, ever-varying, never-ceasing nightmare of his opium-dreams. On this subject he has left us many pages, blending records of his own dreams with such a science or philosophy of opium-dreaming in general as perhaps no other man ever attempted. Biographically, the following is the substance : —That faculty of day-dreaming, of projecting optical images or fancies out of one's own mind into the air, which is con-stitutionally strong in some, and which had been unusually strong in De Quincey from his infancy, was now intensified by his opium-eating into an ungovernable propensity. Especially at night, as he lay awake in bed, his thoughts translated themselves into visions which could not be dismissed, or visions would come of themselves, in the form of " vast processions " and " friezes of never-ending stories " painted on the darkness. This morbid activity of the faculty of visual creation pursued him into sleep. It seemed as if a theatre were "suddenly opened and lighted up" within his brain, for the performance, regularly as sleep came, of nightly extravaganzas and phantasmagories. What had troubled the phantasy already by day would reappear in the night with wonderful transmutations and expansions, or any subject that had been thought of by day would present itself at night in amazing dream-scenery and allegory. But, on the whole, the resources of material for the repeated nightly pageant seemed boundless. What should come, or whence it came, was incalculable. It was as if among the specific potencies of opium was that of searching out whatever was stored up and dormant any-how in the most secret intricacies of the nervous organism, unlocking all doors, compelling all the hoarded photographic impressions of all that had happened in the life of a human being from the hour of birth to yesterday, all that had gone into oblivion with himself and was known to God only, to flash out again, and become real and signifi-cant once more in the dreamy revel. But it was also as if, with all this recovery of the forgotten actual, the bounds of ordinary sense-experience were burst, and the world of the dreams was not the human world, but some other, infernal or supernal. The sense of space, and latterly the sense of time, were strangely affected. One moved, or hung, or sank, in measureless chasms, unshored astronomical abysses, or depths without a star ; minutes shot out into years, or centuries were shrivelled into minutes. When the dream-scenery was most earthly, there was never any comfort in it, but always a sense of misery, dread, struggle and battle, eternal pursuit of something, or eternal flight from some unescapable enemy. He gives specimens of some of the dreams that were most frequent or most hideous. Sometimes, in some recollection of the Malay, the dream-imagery was Oriental, Egypt adding her horrors to those of China and Hindostan, and all three yielding a monstrous jumble of things animate and inanimate, amid which he was compelled to move and suffer, seeking refuge in vain in pagodas and their most secret rooms, or chased for ages through tropical forests, or buried in caves with mummies and sphinxes and all the abominations of the ibis and the crocodile. At other times, though the dream-scenery at first might be Oriental or Alpine, or of grave-yards in some quiet valley, it would turn at last into multitudinous and lamp-lit London, with its mazes and labyrinths of streets, and through those mazes and labyrinths he would himself be wandering round and round, amid legions of ruffianly faces, groping in vain for the lost Ann of Oxford Street.

To wake day after day at noon from such night-mare miseries and be aware of his wife and children standing by him, and to know that, when the day waned, it would only be to plunge him again into the hideous tumult of his other or opium-generated existence, became an agony unsufferable. He shrank from the approach of sleep, and longed to sleep no more. His condition in his waking hours was that of a " suicidal despondency ;" there seemed no exit from his wretchedness ,but suicide or lunacy. At last, however,—just when the reader is tired of the monotony of so much misery, and pity is passing into something like disgust, especially in recollection of the young wife and mother who had to be the nurse of her opium-besotted husband, and indeed when one has been taking refuge from the necessity of such disgust in the fancy that matters were not so bad as they are described, and that some of the more hideous opium-dreams were

subsequent constructions of literary genius, in which
fiction was piled upon remembered fact,—just at this point
one is able to leave the ugly sea of storm and confusion,
and to set foot on a landing-place. This we do in the
year 1819. There had, indeed, been a gleam of returning
hope in the previous year. In the very thickest depth of
De Quincey's mental obscuration, when he could attend to
nothing, and had abandoned a certain great philosophical
work, "*De Emendatione Humani Intellectus,*" which he
had projected in imitation of Spinoza, he had been roused
by the receipt, from a friend in Edinburgh, of a copy of
Ricardo's *Principles of Political Economy,* then recently
published. The book fascinated him; he could read and
enjoy it; he admired the author prodigiously; Ricardo
seemed to him the first man who had shot light and
order into what had hitherto been but a "dark chaos of
materials." He was moved even to write, or to dictate to
his wife, thoughts that grew out of his reading. There
had thus grown in his hands the manuscript of a book or
pamphlet entitled "*Prolegomena to all Future Systems of
Political Economy.*" The book had been actually adver-
tised, and arrangements made for printing it, when the
opium-torpor again fell upon him, and the manuscript was
left incomplete. Now, however, in 1819, he shook himself free with more effect. The circumstances are left
shadowy; and it does not seem that it was then, or till a
while later, that he achieved what he calls his "triumph,"
or release for a good while together from his thraldom to
opium. Enough is told, however, to show that, notwith-
standing all the exertions of his gentle wife, the *res
angusta domi* had become so severe in the cottage at
Grasmere that even the opium-torpor had to relax its
hold and permit the master of the household to rise and

F

look about him.  By some immense effort, De Quincey
had moderated his dependence on the drug, and was
looking about him in something like restored capacity for
work, when,—O, bathos from the projected " *De Emendatione Humani Intellectus* " and the " *Prolegomena to all
Future Systems of Political Economy* " !—he was caught
by the Westmoreland Tories and converted into the editor
of their local newspaper.

The *Westmoreland Gazette* had been started in 1818,
during the general election of that year, when Mr.
Brougham had the first of his three unsuccessful contests
for the great northern county.   It was started at Kendal,
on funds raised by gentlemen who were " friends to the
Constitution," to oppose the " infamous levelling doctrines" of Mr. Brougham, and of the local Whig organ
called the *Kendal Chronicle*.  An editor had been procured
from London, but had turned out a failure ;  and about the
middle of 1819 the editorship was offered to De Quincey.
They had offered him a salary of 160*l.* a year ;  but, as
this was to be for the performance of all the duties, and
as that involved residence in Kendal, De Quincey preferred an arrangement by which he was to pay a sub-editor
to do the drudgery at Kendal, keeping the surplus for
himself for his leading articles and supervising editorship
from Grasmere.   The sub-editor whom he engaged would
not take less than two guineas a week, leaving but 50*l.* 16*s.*
for his chief ;  but the proprietors handsomely made up
this sum to 54*l.* 12*s.*, or a complete guinea a week.   Of
all this De Quincey sent a detailed account, in very hopeful terms, to his uncle in India, informing the colonel at
the same time that he had engagements with *Blackwood's
Magazine* and the *Quarterly Review*, which would bring
him 180*l.* a year more, and concluding with a request

to be allowed to draw upon the colonel for 500*l.*, " say 150*l.* now, and the other 350*l.* in six or eight months hence." This would re-establish him for life, he said, and he looked forward to a removal to London, to resume his training for the profession of the law.

The specimens given by Mr. Page, from the files of the *Westmoreland Gazette,* of De Quincey's leading articles and notices to correspondents during his time of editorship, confirm Mr. Page's general conclusion that he " was not born for a successful newspaper editor." Perhaps the most characteristic of the quoted specimens is an article in which, in answer to remonstrances that he was flying over the heads of his readers, he expounds his ideas of provincial editorship in general and of the prospects of the *Westmoreland Gazette* in particular. " The editor " he says " can assure his readers that his own personal friends " in most of the Universities, especially in the three " weightiest,—Oxford, Cambridge, and Edinburgh,—are " quite competent in number and power to float the " *Gazette* triumphantly into every section and division of " those learned bodies." Nor was this all. While not neglecting the demands of his humbler constituents of Westmoreland, he could not forget that well-educated and learned readers were numerous in the county. For their sakes, he is proud to intimate that he " has received " assurances of support from two of the most illustrious " men in point of intellectual pretensions that have ap- " peared for some ages,"—whether Wordsworth and Coleridge, or Wordsworth and Southey, is not quite obvious. But even this is not all. " The editor will go " a step further. He will venture to affirm that, even " without the powerful aid here noticed (to which he " might have added a promise of co-operation from London,

" the four great commercial towns of the second class, many
" of the third class, and so downwards, as also occasion-
" ally from Paris and Vienna, from Canada, and from
" Hindostan, &c.),—even without the powerful aid here
" noticed, he could singly and unsupported secure to the
" *Gazette* one feature of originality which would draw
" upon it a general notice throughout Great Britain."
Was not German Literature a yet unworked mine of
wealth, an absolute Potosi ; and might not the editor say
without vanity, since his part would be only that of
selecting and translating, that no journal in the kingdom
could draw on this mine so easily, or exhibit such nuggets
from it weekly, as the *Westmoreland Gazette ?*—All this
for a guinea a-week to the editor at Grasmere, with two
guineas a week for the grimy cormorant drudging for him
in some public-house at Kendal ! There is something
like evidence, however, that the cormorant was dismissed,
and that De Quincey took up his quarters for some time
at Kendal, uniting the functions of editor and sub-editor,
and, it is to be hoped, their salaries. There is one letter from
him to his wife, at all events, dated " Commercial Inn,
11 o'clock on Thursday night," which presents him as
then in Kendal by himself, before a table covered with
printer's proofs, and very heavy-hearted at being away
from Grasmere. He has been vexed particularly by news
of the illness of his little child Margaret. " God bless
her, poor little lamb ! " he ejaculates affectionately, adding
that, if his wife cannot come to Kendal to-morrow, he
will try to be at Grasmere next week.

After all, De Quincey seems to have done not badly in
his editorship, even by the standard of the Tory gentlemen of Westmoreland. If the local circulation was
not large, the matter administered was probably more

acceptable to the country folks than that of Coleridge's *Friend*. One thing the editorship had done for De Quincey himself. It had given him a liking for the sight of printer's proofs. Accordingly, his editorship of the *Westmoreland Gazette* having come to an end some time in 1820, or been converted, by understanding with the proprietors, into a mere contributorship thenceforward, he was on the outlook for other literary employment. Not unnaturally, his thoughts turned first to Edinburgh, where his friend Wilson, now Professor of Moral Philosophy, had since 1817 been the lord of *Blackwood's Magazine*, and he and Lockhart and a band of daring young Tories about them had made that magazine at once a terror and a new splendour in the island, and where there was no lack of other literary possibilities and openings. The engagement on *Blackwood* mentioned by De Quincey to his uncle in 1819 had, it would appear, turned out a quasi-engagement only; and in the end of 1820 he is found in Edinburgh in person, examining chances on the spot. In a letter to his wife thence, dated Dec. 9, 1820, he speaks of the cordial reception he has had among his old Edinburgh friends. Nothing definite, however, seems to have come of the visit. Wilson, one cannot doubt, did his best; but there may have been difficulties. And so, not yet an actual contributor to *Blackwood*, but only a potential contributor, De Quincey was back at his home in the Lakes early in 1821. It was in London, and not in Edinburgh, that he was first to appear as a writer in Magazines.

# CHAPTER VII.

PARTLY IN LONDON, PARTLY AT THE LAKES, PARTLY IN
EDINBURGH : THE "CONFESSIONS" AND OTHER ARTICLES
IN THE "LONDON MAGAZINE," AND FIRST ARTICLES IN
"BLACKWOOD."

## 1821—1830.

THE metropolitan magazine of chief note in those days
was *The London Magazine.* It had been established in
January 1820, with Messrs. Baldwin, Cradock, and Co., for
the publishers, and the Aberdonian Mr. John Scott for
editor ; but, in July 1821, after the death of Scott in his
unfortunate duel, it passed into the hands of Messrs.
Taylor and Hessey, who were thenceforward themselves
the editors. And very good editors they were. Aiming
high, and having retained the best of the contributors in
Scott's time and added others, they had already, in 1821,
a sufficiently remarkable staff about them, whom they
kept in good humour and a kind of stimulated unity of
endeavour, not only by what was then considered liberal
pay, but also by an excellent monthly dinner, for talk
and wit-combat, at the expense of the firm. Keats, who
had contributed verses to the earlier numbers, had died in
February 1821 ; but Charles Lamb, at the age of forty-
six, and under his newly adopted signature of "Elia,"
was obliging Messrs. Taylor and Hessey, and the world,
with fresh specimens of his charming Essays. Among

the other contributors were, or were to be, Hazlitt, John
Hamilton Reynolds, the stalwart Allan Cunningham,
the Rev. Henry Francis Cary, John Poole, George Darley,
Bryan Waller Procter, and Thomas Hood. This last, indeed, at the age of twenty-three, was a kind of assistant-
editor. There was also a certain shabby-genteel and
bejewelled effeminate, named Thomas Griffith Wainwright, whose department was the Fine Arts, and who,
under the signature of " Janus Weathercock," wrote most
of the articles on great painters and engravers, and criticisms of contemporary pictures. He was to die in
Australia long afterwards as a convict who had been
transported for forgery, but who was known also, by
evidence irresistible, as the murderer, by poison, of two
young ladies, boarders in his house, on whose lives he had
speculated for a total of 18,000*l.* by scattered investments
in different insurance-offices.

It is curious to look over the old volumes of the *London
Magazine* now, and to observe the papers in them that
have become classic. It was in the number for September
1821, or about two months after Messrs. Taylor and
Hessey had become proprietors, that there appeared a
paper of twenty pages entitled *Confessions of an Opium-
Eater, being an Extract from the Life of a Scholar*. That
there were unusual expectations of popularity for this
piece is proved by the appended editorial note ( ? by
young Hood), stating that " the remainder of this very
interesting article will be given in the next number."
Accordingly, the number for October 1821 leads off
with Part II. of the *Confessions* in 27 pages. It contains, moreover, a notice from the author explanatory of
the dates in the First Part, and another editorial paragraph
of congratulation over the new contributor. " We are

" not often in the habit of eulogizing our own work," says
the paragraph ; " but we cannot neglect the opportunity
" which the following explanatory note gives us of calling
" the attention of our readers to the deep, eloquent, and
" masterly paper which stands first in our present number."
The *Confessions*, in fact, were widely read, and roused
much curiosity. The cry, on all hands, was for more of
the same extraordinary matter. That was not so easy ;
but in the number for December 1821 there appeared a
letter from the Opium-Eater, signed " X.Y.Z.," courteously
rebuking Mr. James Montgomery for his scepticism as to
the authenticity of the *Confessions*, and promising a Third
Part in time. Meanwhile, in the same number, the public
had from the new author, signing himself "Grasmeriensis
Teutonizans," a paper *On the Writings of John Paul
Frederick Richter*, including a translated specimen. Then,
for a whole year, there was a break, the promise of a continuation of the *Confessions* hanging unfulfilled, and the
readers of the magazine having to content themselves with
other fare, the best morsel of which was Charles Lamb's
"Dissertation on Roast Pig" in September 1822. In
that year, 1822, however, Messrs. Taylor and Hessey had
the pleasure of bringing out the *Confessions of an English
Opium-Eater* in a separate little duodecimo volume, the
author's name still suppressed. They would fain still
have had the promised continuation in their magazine,
and apologized to their readers for not having been able to
fulfil that engagement. By way of compensation, they
were glad to publish, through the years 1823 and 1824,
everything that De Quincey chose to give them, taking
care that it should be known that the articles were by
" The English Opium-Eater."

In January 1823 were begun *Letters to a Young Man*

*whose Education has been neglected,* continued in the
numbers for February, March, May, and June; in the
April number, which these " Letters " had skipped, appeared a sketch of Herder under the title *The Death of a
German Great Man* ; and, not to mention less important
contributions straggling through the numbers of the year,
the September number contained the first instalment, and
the October and November numbers two more instalments,
of the series of papers entitled generally *Notes from the
Pocket-Book of a late Opium-Eater,* and sub-titled individually " Walking Stewart," " Malthus, " On the Knocking at the Gate in Macbeth," " English Dictionaries," &c.
In December 1823 an *Answer of the Opium-Eater to Mr.
Hazlitt's Letter respecting Mr. Malthus,* and a paper *On
Malthus's Measure of Value,* made the public further aware
of the Opium-Eater's pretensions in Political Economy.—
The year 1824 was not less prolific. The January number
for that year gave the first part of the Opium-Eater's
*Historico-Critical Inquiry into the Origin of the Rosicru-
cians and Freemasons,* continued in February and March
and not concluded till June ; the February·number gave
also *Analects from John Paul Richter,* in the form of five
more translated specimens of that author ; the March number gave, as an additional specimen of Richter, his *Dream
upon the Universe ;* and in various numbers from March
to July there were further instalments of *Notes from the
Pocket-Book of a late Opium-Eater.* Thus we arrive at
the months of August and September 1824, made
memorable by a special contribution from the Opium-
Eater. Another British pioneer of German Literature had
recently appeared in Mr. Thomas Carlyle, ten years younger
than De Quincey, and of limited reputation as yet. His
translation of Goethe's *Wilhelm Meister* had just been

published anonymously in Edinburgh; and, having been recommended to the *London Magazine* by Edward Irving, he was breaking up, to be sent from Scotland, for anonymous publication in that magazine, his *Life of Schiller*, then in manuscript. The first portion of the Life had appeared in the number for October 1823; the second portion had appeared in the number for January 1824, along with the first instalment of De Quincey's Rosicrucian Inquiry; the third had appeared in July 1824 (Carlyle then on his first visit to London); and the remainder came out in August and September. It was rather hard that in those very two numbers there should appear De Quincey's article on Goethe, founded on his fellow-contributor's *Translation of Wilhelm Meister*. In the main, it is true, the article was an onslaught on Goethe himself, an attempt to drag him down from the eminence claimed for him by his translator and others, and to represent him as a tedious and immoral old impostor; but the translator came in for a share of the blame. He was taken to task for his Scotticisms, his mistakes in the German, and generally for the stiffness and awkwardness of his English prose. Altogether the critique was, as Carlyle has owned, a rather annoying log of offence thrown across his path at that moment. After the article on Goethe, De Quincey's contributions to the magazine in 1824 were *Walladmor: Analysis of a German Novel*, and a translation of Kant's *Idea of a Universal History on a Cosmopolitical Plan*, both in the October number, and a paper entitled *Falsification of the History of England*, which appeared in the number for December.

The connexion of De Quincey with the *London Magazine* seems to have ceased after 1824, in consequence of arrangements about that time by Messrs. Taylor and

Hessey for quitting the proprietorship.  But others were
on the alert for anything from the pen of " The Opium-
Eater."   Mr. Charles Knight, who had started his
" Knight's Quarterly Magazine " in 1823, and who counted
the brilliant young Macaulay and the brilliant young Praed on
his staff, had obtained at least one article from De Quincey,
and had become personally acquainted with him in July
1824, with a view to more.  But a good deal of De Quincey's
time in the year 1825 was taken up with a wretched
piece of literary business into which he had been lured by
his own analysis of the German novel *Walladmor* in the
*London Magazine* of October 1824.   The said *Walladmor*
was a German fabrication, in the shape of a pretended
" New Romance by the Author of Waverley," brought out
at Leipsic at a time when there was a lull in the production of those real Waverley Novels without which German
readers, as well as British, found life insipid.   Germany
was deceived from end to end by the three-volume substitute for the absent reality.   The first copy imported into
England having come into De Quincey's hands, he had
scribbled his article on it for the magazine as rapidly as
he could, with the unfortunate effect that, having hit on
some passages of merit and translated them, he was
commissioned by Messrs. Taylor and Hessey to translate
the whole.   When he became better acquainted with the
rubbish, he would gladly have been free from the task ;
but, as that could not be, he took his revenge by treating
the affair as a practical joke.   He so cut and carved
the original, and De Quinceyfied it by insertions and
compressions, as to be able to bring out, in the course of
1825, an English *Walladmor* in two volumes, with a
prefixed " dedication " of elaborate banter.

And so, from  1821 to 1825, or  between De Quincey's

thirty-seventh and his forty-first year, we have the first burst of his magazine articles and cognate publications. If he had come late into the field of literature, he had come into it at last with one advantage. There had been immense, if unintended, preparation; De Quincey's articles, like George Eliot's novels afterwards, had not to be spun out of a vacuum. There can be no doubt, however, that De Quincey's sudden leap into celebrity was due in great part to the peculiar nature of the articles by which he had chosen to introduce himself. There was something almost staggering in the act of self-exposure by which a man consented that he should be known as "The Opium-Eater," not figuratively or fictitiously, as some at first supposed, but with the most positive assurances that his revelations were real excerpts from his own life. The signature of "The Opium-Eater" to any article whatever became thenceforward an attraction. Not that this would have lasted long had there not been recompense in super-lative measure in the articles themselves. But who could deny that there was such recompense? Here, evidently, was no common writer, no dullard or hack, but a new man of genius, a new power in English Prose Literature. There was proclamation of the fact in a quarter whence a favourable verdict was then of some value. As early as October 1823 "The Opium-Eater" had been made to figure as a colloquist in Wilson's *Noctes Ambrosianæ*; and again, in October 1825, there was a passage in the *Noctes* praising De Quincey as "a man of a million." This, of course, was kindness on Wilson's part; but it was no exaggeration of the current opinion.

What meanwhile, through the four years of his growing celebrity, had De Quincey himself been doing? Though Grasmere was still his nominal headquarters (where indeed his books and papers had by this time overflowed his own cottage at Townend, and invaded his father-in-law's cottage of Rydal Nab, if not a third cottage adjacent), the clear inference from the records is that from 1821 to 1825 he resided chiefly in London. There is a very interesting note on the subject, though with some exaggeration of the fact, in Bohn's edition of Lowndes's *Bibliographer's Manual.* "The *Confessions,*" Mr. Bohn says, " were written in a " little room at the back of Mr. H. G. Bohn's premises, " No. 4, York Street, Covent Garden, where Mr. De " Quincey resided, in comparative seclusion, for several " years. He had previously lived in the neighbourhood " of Soho Square, and for some years was a frequent " visitor to the shop of Mr. Bohn's father, then the " principal dealer in German books. The writer remembers " that he always seemed to speak in a kind of whisper." From De Quincey's own reminiscences we gather some other particulars. It was during the time of his connexion with the *London Magazine* that he came thoroughly to know Lamb and his sister and saw most of them. They were excessively kind to him, insisting on his coming from his solitary lodgings as often as possible to dine and spend the evening with them ; and he describes some of those quiet evenings with the Lambs very tenderly and prettily, testifying the increase of his regard for the good brother and sister the more he knew of their heroic relations to each other, and of their real benevolence. He does not seem to have been frequently at the monthly dinners given by Messrs. Taylor and Hessey to their magazine staff, and at which Lamb, as the chief of the wits round the table, always stuttered and sparkled at his brightest. Barry Cornwall could remember De Quincey's appearance at only one of those dinners, when " the

expression of his face was intelligent, but cramped and
somewhat peevish," and when he "was self-involved and
did not add to the cheerfulness of the meeting." This
may have been at the particular dinner of November 1821
at which, as De Quincey tells us himself, he met Mr.
Wainwright among the company, did not like him, and
rather wondered why Lamb paid him so much attention.
Walks with Hazlitt and little angry discussions with him,
and glimpses of young Talfourd and other lights rising or
risen on the skirts of Messrs. Taylor and Hessey's literary
group, are also to be imagined. The sub-editorial calls at
his lodgings by young Thomas Hood, on the "frequent
and agreeable duty" of dunning him for copy, must not
be forgotten. Then it was, as Hood liked to remember in
after-years, that he used to find De Quincey "in the midst
of a German Ocean of Literature," his room flooded and
plugged with books, and that, invited sometimes to stay,
he would listen with amazement to the strange tenant of
the rooms far into the small hours. He still retained a
memento of those visits, he adds, in the original manuscript
of one of De Quincey's papers, exhibiting the stain of "a
large purplish ring" where the tumbler of laudanum
negus had rested on it. For, in his London solitude, and
apparently in 1823-4, the author of the *Confessions*, who
had signified that the days of his opium-eating were past,
had again succumbed. What with this relapse into his
old habit, what with the constant depression of his ill-
health, he was again very wretched ; and the picture we
have to form of him in those days from all the preserved
memorials is the very reverse of that which would have
been natural in any other case of such suddenly attained
literary distinction. Not as a lion in general society or as
a frequenter of club-dinners, or even as a man at home of

his own accord in the houses of a few select friends, is the De Quincey of 1821—1825 to be figured, but rather as the confirmed and incurable eccentric, the incarnation of shy nervousness, that he was to be for all the rest of his life. He avoided intercourse with his fellow-creatures as much as he could, and was happy, if he was ever happy, only in solitary afternoon walks about Covent Garden and the Strand, where he could observe passers-by and look into shop-windows, or in longer rambles at night out into un- known suburbs, whence he could return, by silent circuits of roads, to his own book-blocked room and the laudanum negus.

Now, as afterwards, friends and admirers who desired his intimacy had, as it were, to break in upon him. We do hear of one or two such friendly inroads on his comfortless privacy. Thus, in the summer of 1824, Mr. Matthew Davenport Hill sought him out, and roused him not a little. More effective still seems to have been Mr. Charles Knight's acquaintanceship with him, begun, as we have seen, in the interests of "Knight's Quarterly Magazine." Mr. Knight, six years younger than De Quincey, and ardent in literature in those days with even more than the usual ardour of a young publisher, liked nothing better than to get De Quincey to dine with him, or stay with him a while, in his house in Pall Mall East. "O! for an hour of De Quincey!" he wrote years after- wards, in recollection of those evenings in comparison with any he had spent in the interval; and he has handed down several anecdotes illustrative of the incredible helplessness of the little guest whom he and his household so liked to shelter. One day in 1825, Mr. Knight, returning from Windsor, found that De Quincey, whom he had left in his house in Pall Mall East, had departed abruptly, leaving

word that he had gone home to Westmoreland. Knowing
that he had intended to go thither, and had only been
waiting for a remittance from his mother to " satisfy
some clamorous creditors " before he went, Mr. Knight
thought nothing of the matter. In a few days, however,
he heard that De Quincey was still in town and in a
dreadful difficulty. Following the clue to his whereabouts,
he found him in a miserable lodging on the Surrey side of
the river, his " dreadful difficulty " being that the expected
remittance had reached him in the form of a large draft
on a London bank payable at twenty-one days' sight, and
that he had been informed, on going to Lombard Street,
that the draft could not be cashed till the time was up.
Too shy to return to Mr. Knight's house and explain why
he had come back, he had gone, for accommodation for the
twenty-one days, into a hiding-hole where he was really not
safe from being robbed ; and it was with surprise, as well
as delight, that he received Mr. Knight's assurance that the
difficulty about the draft was not insuperable, and he
might have the cash at once.

Mr. Knight's anecdote fits in but too well with other
proofs that one of the causes of De Quincey's moping and
evasive habits through the time of his London life was
excruciating pecuniary embarrassment. And no wonder.
The calculation even now is that a writer for magazines
and reviews can hardly, by his utmost industry, unless he
is also on the staff of a newspaper, or is exceptionally
retained by a fixed engagement, as Southey and Macaulay
were, make more than 250*l.* a year. On that hypothesis
it is not difficult to compute that all De Quincey's earnings
between 1821 and 1825, by the *London Magazine* or whatever else, must have been a poor provision for the expenses
of himself in London and of his family at Grasmere. In

fact, however it happened, he was so much in debt, and so hard pressed for money, as to be on this account also desperately miserable. "At this time," he had written to Professor Wilson in Edinburgh on the 24th of February, 1825, "I am quite free from opium; but it has left the "liver, the Achilles' heel of almost every human fabric, "subject to affections which are tremendous for the weight "of wretchedness attached to them. To fence with these "with the one hand, and with the other to maintain the "war with the wretched business of hack-author, with "all its horrible degradations, is more than I am able "to bear. At this moment I have not a place to hide "my head in. Something I meditate,—I know not what ". . . With a good publisher and leisure to premeditate "what I write, I might yet liberate myself: after which, "having paid everybody, I would slink into some dark "corner, educate my children, and show my face in the "world no more." He adds that he may be addressed either "to the care of Mrs. De Quincey, Rydal Nab, Westmoreland," or "to the care of M. D. Hill, Esq., 11, King's Bench Walk, Temple," but that the latter address might be the better, because he would rather not be tracked too precisely at present. Perhaps it was the "large draft" of Mr. Knight's anecdote that cleared the way for the desired return to Westmoreland. Not at this point only in De Quincey's biography has the reader to suspect "remittances from his mother" of which there is no distinct record.

De Quincey was certainly back in Westmoreland before the end of 1825, and in circumstances tolerably easy after his late London experience. "Thank God you are not now domineered over by circumstances, and may your noble nature never more be disturbed but by its own workings!"

we find Wilson writing to him from Edinburgh on the 12th
November in that year. The letter, which begins "My
dear Plato," speaks of promised contributions by De
Quincey to a forthcoming volume of miscellanies which
Wilson and Lockhart had projected, under the name
of "Janus, or the Edinburgh Literary Almanac." It
also adverts to Lockhart's commencing editorship of the
*Quarterly Review*, and to the interest De Quincey may
have in that event. "He knows your great talents,
and will, I know, act in the most gentlemanly spirit to
all contributors"; and why should not De Quincey be
thinking of a noble article on Kant for the new editor?

Though "Janus" had to appear in the beginning of
1826 without De Quincey's hand in it, Wilson's letter
prepares us for the next important stage in his literary life.
This was his connexion, through Wilson, with *Blackwood's Magazine*. It began by the publication in the
number of that magazine for November 1826 of the first
portion of an article on Lessing, entitled *Lessing's Laocoon,
translated with Notes*. The second portion appeared in
the number for January 1827, and was followed in
February 1827 by *The Last Days of Immanuel Kant*
and the famous essay *On Murder considered as one of the
Fine Arts;* and in March 1827 appeared the paper
entitled *Toilette of the Hebrew Lady*. After an interval,
i.e. in August 1830, there was another paper on Kant,
entitled *Kant in his Miscellaneous Essays*.

The connexion with *Blackwood* very naturally drew
De Quincey himself once more to Edinburgh. Accordingly,
through the years 1827, 1828, and 1829, we find him
quite as much in Edinburgh as at Grasmere. He was, of
course, no stranger there, but moved about familiarly
among such surviving friends of his former visits as were

still resident in the city. Wilson was his mainstay, the man who had known him longest and understood him best, and whose own joviality of disposition made it easier for him than it would have been for most to tolerate the eccentricities of such a weird little son of genius and opium. Wilson's house in Gloucester Place was at De Quincey's disposal when he liked ; and one of the best sketches of De Quincey is that by Wilson's daughter, Mrs. Gordon, in her life of her father, where she gives her recollections of the Opium-Eater's troublesome irregularities of habit in the house, the cook's difficulties with him and profound reverence for him, and all the while Wilson's magnanimous laugh at the whole concern. It was at this time too, and indirectly through Wilson, that Carlyle first saw something of De Quincey personally. They met, I think, at the house of one of Wilson's friends ; after which there were calls from De Quincey at Comely Bank, where Carlyle and his wife had their Edinburgh home between their marriage in 1826 and their removal to the Dumfries-shire solitude of Craigenputtock in 1828. At first, De Quincey, remembering his review of Carlyle's Translation of Wilhelm Meister, was obviously ill at ease ; but, that matter left unmentioned, the meetings seem to have been pleasant enough on both sides. That Carlyle's interest in De Quincey, at all events, was far from small at this time is proved by his long letter from Craigenputtock, of December 11, 1828, inviting De Quincey to visit him and his wife there. " Our warmest welcome, and such solacements as even the desert does not refuse," Carlyle writes, " are at any time and at all times in store for one we love so well " ; and, after a humorous description of a possible colony or social college of like-minded spirits on the moors round Craigenputtock, there is the complimentary addition, " Would *you* come hither and be king over us, then indeed we had made a fair beginning, and the *Bog School* might snap its fingers at the *Lake School*." Nearer the end of the letter came these significant words, " Believe it, you are well loved here, and none feels better than I what a spirit is for the present eclipsed in clouds. For the present it can only be ; time and chance are for all men ; that troublous season will end." Evidently De Quincey's troubles of various kinds were clinging to him in Edinburgh, and Carlyle knew all.

The pecuniary trouble, for one, had not ceased. It was a great thing, doubtless, to be a writer in *Blackwood ;* but a few articles in that magazine in the course of four years could not do much toward the support of the man of letters in Edinburgh and of his wife and young ones in the Vale of Grasmere. There was income, doubtless, from other sources,—perhaps from periodicals in London ; perhaps from newspapers ; and certainly from the *Edinburgh Literary Gazette,* a weekly periodical then of some note in Edinburgh, to which De Quincey contributed occasionally through 1828, 1829, and 1830. But the deficit altogether must have been serious and growing. What was the remedy ? Poor as the pastures in Edinburgh were, they were better than were likely to be found anywhere else. His chief existing engagements were there ; and nowhere else did farther engagements seem so easy. Why, then, keep up two households, or pretences of a household, one in Edinburgh and one in Westmoreland ? Why should not Mrs. De Quincey and her children leave their native vale and be domiciled with De Quincey permanently in Edinburgh ? Both De Quincey and his wife were adverse to the idea of leaving Grasmere ; but at length, in 1830, apparently on the spur of some new offer of literary engagement in Edinburgh, the resolution was taken. It was precipitated by the advice of the excellent and sensible Dorothy Wordsworth. In a long letter of Dorothy's to De Quincey, giving him an account of a visit she had paid to his cottage just after her return to Rydal Mount from a tour, she tells him she had found his wife well, but "with something of sadness in her manner" when she spoke of the likelihood of his detention in Edinburgh by a certain new engagement of which she had heard vaguely. Dorothy's reply, she informs De Quincey, had been "Why not settle there, for the time at least that this engagement lasts? Lodgings are cheap in Edinburgh, and provisions and coals not dear." Mrs. De Quincey, having acquiesced, had asked Dorothy to write on the subject to De Quincey; and hence her letter. She there repeats her advice in greater detail, with all delicacy but very practically. The first step taken in the direction of the advice seems to have been the removal of the elder children from Grasmere to Edinburgh; but in 1830 Mrs. De Quincey and the younger children followed. The cottage in Grasmere was nominally retained as De Quincey's for some years more; but from 1830 Edinburgh, and Edinburgh all but alone, was to contain him and his, and their united fortunes, so long as he remained in the world. He was then forty-five years of age, and his wife about two and thirty.

# CHAPTER VIII.

WHOLLY IN EDINBURGH : MORE CONTRIBUTIONS TO "BLACK-
WOOD," WITH ARTICLES IN "TAIT'S MAGAZINE."
1830—1840.

EDINBURGH from 1830 to 1840 was a very excellent place
of residence.  The indestructible natural beauties of her
site and surroundings, the extraordinary combination of
dense and antique picturesqueness with modern elegance
and spaciousness in the plan and architecture of her
streets and slopes, and the wealth of her interesting traditions from the past, were not her only recommendations.
A pleasant and varied social activity still characterized
her as the metropolis of Scotland, and an unusual number
of persons of greater or less note individually moved
among her 130,000 or 150,000 inhabitants.  Her greatest
man, it is true, was lost to her in 1832, when Scott died,
and heads could no longer be turned to look at his vene-
rated figure as he limped along Princes Street.  But
Jeffrey remained, Lord Advocate of Scotland from 1830
to 1834, and thenceforward a Judge with the title of Lord
Jeffrey, only ex-editor of the *Edinburgh Review* now, and
not writing much more, but still the literary pride of the
Edinburgh Whigs.  Wilson, on the other hand, as the
"Christopher North" of *Blackwood* and the eloquent and
adored University Professor, was in his most exuberant
prime, Scott's successor, so far as there was one, in the

literary chiefship of Edinburgh Toryism, and the observed of all observers, Whig or Tory, for his lion-like gait and gesture, wild yellow hair, and frequent white hat. Then, among Jeffrey's colleagues or subordinates in the Parliament House, or Wilson's associates in the University, or belonging to both fraternities, or distributed in divers posts and professions through the city, what a miscellany of other local celebrities ! Among the lawyers, on the bench or rising to it, were Moncreiff, Cockburn, Patrick Robertson, Rutherfurd, Ivory, and Murray. Among the University Professors, in one or other of the faculties, were Sir William Hamilton (first in the chair of History, and after 1836 in that of Logic and Metaphysics), Dr. Chalmers (brought to Edinburgh in 1828 as Professor of Theology), Dunbar, Pillans, Welsh, Macvey Napier, Jameson, Hope, Monro *tertius*, Sir Charles Bell, Pulteney Alison, Syme, Christison, and (from 1835) George Moir. Conspicuous in science or in medicine out of the University were Dr. Abercrombie, Sir David Brewster, Andrew and George Combe, and others. McCrie, the biographer of Knox, was alive for part of the time ; before the ten years were out Candlish and Guthrie were in their Edinburgh pulpits ; and those who preferred milder or Episcopalian pastorship could " sit under " the Rev. E. B. Ramsay, afterwards Dean Ramsay, or the Rev. Robert Morehead. There was a flourishing Edinburgh theatre, with the accomplished Mr. Murray as manager and one of the actors, and with Mackay as the non-such in " Bailie Nicol Jarvie," " Caleb Balderstone," and other comic characters in the dramas from Scott's novels. Among resident representatives of the Fine Arts were Sir William Allan, Watson Gordon, Harvey, Duncan, and the recluse and abstruse David Scott ; and among resi-

dent, or all but resident, representatives of literature not already mentioned, most of them lawyers and in training for
legal posts or professorships, were Thomas Thomson, Sir
Thomas Dick Lauder, David Laing, Charles Kirkpatrick
Sharpe, David Macbeth Moir, Henry Glassford Bell,
Archibald Alison, William and Robert Chambers, Ferrier,
Spalding, Thomas Aird, Hill Burton, John Thomson
Gordon, and William Edmonstoune Aytoun. Lady Nairne,
the woman of finest lyric genius Scotland has produced,
unless Lady Wardlaw may be compared with her, was
living in the near vicinity, her claims to authorship
of any kind as yet undivulged; and the best-known
literary ladies of Edinburgh were Miss Ferrier and Mrs.
Johnstone. The chief newspapers were the *Scotsman*,
edited by Mr. Charles Maclaren, and the *Caledonian
Mercury*, edited by Dr. James Browne; and the two
editors had fought a duel. An event of real importance
was the foundation of *Chambers's Edinburgh Journal* by
Messrs. William and Robert Chambers in 1832, super-
seding the previous literary weeklies of the city, and
setting the example of cheapness for all future British
periodicals. The Reform Bill agitation for some time,
and then the other agitations that grew out of that, provided political hot water in abundance for the ten years;
and in no community was the supply kept at a higher
temperature. If you lived in Edinburgh between 1830
and 1840, you must be a Whig or a Tory; on one or
other of those two stools you were compelled to sit, as by
a law of human existence; they would not permit you to
try both, or to stand, or to walk about. Further, as the
mere mention of the name of Dr. Chalmers will have
suggested, that was the time of this great man's energetic
leadership in the ecclesiastical politics of Scotland, and of

the beginnings of that ecclesiastical strife which, manifesting itself more fiercely from year to year in the annual
General Assemblies of the Kirk in Edinburgh, had its
final issue in 1843 in the disruption of the Scottish
Establishment.

Such was the Edinburgh within which the English
eccentric and visionary was enclosed from his forty-sixth
year to his fifty-sixth. We know now what to think of
him in his relations to the community in which he had
sought refuge. If we set aside Dr. Chalmers, a really
great man, cast in nature's largest mould, but not specially
a man of letters, and if we set aside also Sir William
Hamilton, as less the man of letters than the scholastic
thinker, then in all Edinburgh, after Scott's death,
with due exception for the uncombed strength and bar-
baric word-splendours of Christopher North, the most
important intellectual figure was the shy little English
stranger. It was De Quincey that the real lovers of
literature in Edinburgh ought to have sought out, if they
wanted to put the very rarest they had amongst them on
a pedestal in front of the Register House, to be publicly
saluted and gazed at. They did nothing of the kind. It
was not known to the vast majority of the inhabitants of
Edinburgh that anybody of the name of De Quincey was
living among them ; and even the young lovers of literature that knew a little about him all but invariably mis-
spelt his name when they wrote it or printed it. The
reasons are pretty obvious. Merely as an Englishman,
De Quincey was somewhat out of his element. He was
in Edinburgh, but not of Edinburgh, a little put out by
the Scottish "*Saw*bath," as he used to write it jocularly,
and by cognate observances (though in this he had native
sympathizers), and not in touch with any part of the

municipal tumult around him. But much more was his
social insignificance owing to the fact that he was simply
De Quincey. By temperament and habit he was a creature
evasive of all publicity, a "fantastical duke of dark
corners"; and he had seen too many specimens of literary
eminence already, in Wordsworth, Coleridge, and others,
to have much passion left for such new literary acquain-
tanceships as Edinburgh might afford. In fact, he did
not care very much where he was, if only people would
not ask him out to dinner, but would leave him alone
with his books, his manuscripts, and his opium.

The literary industry of De Quincey through the ten
years is represented mainly by the list of his continued
contributions to *Blackwood*, and by a series of contributions to another Edinburgh monthly, called *Tait's Magazine*. In *Blackwood* for 1831 appeared *Dr. Parr and
his Contemporaries, or Whiggism in its Relations to
Literature;* in the same magazine, under the title of *The
Cæsars*, there was begun, in October 1832, a series of
articles on Roman History which extended over four subsequent numbers; in November 1832 appeared the article
entitled *Charlemagne;* and in April 1833 appeared *The
Revolution of Greece*. There was then an interruption of
four years; but in July 1837 appeared the long narrative
paper called *Revolt of the Tartars;* which was followed
in 1838 by *Household Wreck* and *Modern Greece*, and in
1839 by *Casuistry* and *Dinner, Real and Reputed*. The
year 1840 was marked by the production of the series of
papers entitled *The Essenes*, the articles entitled *Alleged
Plagiarisms of Coleridge* and *Modern Superstition*, and
the series on *Style and Rhetoric*.—Meanwhile De Quincey
had been contributing also to *Tait*, a magazine which had
been started by an Edinburgh bookseller in 1832 on

advanced Whig principles in politics, but perfectly open
and unfettered in all literary respects. It was in February
1834, just at the time of the break with *Blackwood* noted
above, that *Tait* began to astonish its readers by *Sketches
of Life and Manners from the Autobiography of an English Opium-Eater*. The series ran on, sometimes with
explanatory sub-titles, through the rest of 1834 and
through 1835 and 1836; and, even after the connexion
with *Blackwood* was resumed in 1837, *Tait* was able
to entertain its readers for three years more with new
instalments of the same. The Sketches, indeed, extending over about thirty articles in all, contain that Autobiography of De Quincey the republished portions of
which in the English edition of his Collected Works form,
together with *The Confessions*, the most frequently read
volumes of the collection. No portions of the series
attracted greater attention at the time, or excited more
wrath in certain quarters, than the digressions upon the
recently dead Coleridge and the still living Wordsworth
and Southey. Carlyle has told us how Southey in particular, when he first met him, flamed up on the mention
of De Quincey's name, averring that it would be but a
proper service to good manners if some one were to go to
Edinburgh and thrash the little wretch; and we hear
elsewhere of the offence taken also by the Wordsworths
and by members of the Coleridge family. Yet, as Carlyle
seems to have thought, the complaints were excessive.
The amount of personal gossip in the papers was much less
than we have been accustomed to since; the "vivisec-
tion," what little there was of it, was avowedly for scientific
purposes; and no one could deny the generosity of the
general estimates. The admiration expressed for Coleridge and Wordsworth all in all, indeed, went beyond

what the world even then was willing to accord; and it may be doubted whether we have yet in our literature any more interesting accounts of the philosopher and the poet than those admiring, but sharp-sighted, papers. They and the rest of the articles in the same series were, at all events, most acceptable when they appeared in the pages of *Tait*. There were, however, contributions of an independent kind to the same pages, the most important being *A Tory's Account of Toryism, Whiggism, and Radicalism*, in 1835 and 1836. The average amount of De Quincey's contributions to the two magazines jointly through the ten years was about six articles every year. During the same period he wrote the articles *Goethe, Pope, Shakespeare*, and *Schiller*, for the seventh edition of the Encyclopædia Britannica, edited by Mr. Macvey Napier; and there may have been other contributions to minor periodicals. Moreover, during the same period he had produced one of the only two specimens of his powers given to the world originally in the book form. This was his *Klosterheim, or the Masque*, a romance, published by Blackwood, in a duodecimo volume, in 1832.

De Quincey's domestic life in Edinburgh through a period of such marked literary industry is involved in considerable obscurity. We learn incidentally that he was a guest in Wilson's house in Gloucester Place for some time continuously in 1830-31; we hear of a largish furnished house or set of apartments in Great King Street taken by him for himself and his family in 1831; and we hear further that there were removals to Forres Street, still in the New Town, and to the village of Duddingston, an outskirt of the Old Town, at the back of Arthur Seat. Perhaps there were other shiftings and burrowings. In general, all that is clear is that there was

a succession of domiciles, with always one room in each
where, amidst a chaos of books and papers on the floor,
chairs, and tables, the indefatigable little scholar could
pursue his studies, penning his articles, one after another,
in his peculiarly neat small hand, on the little bit of space
kept free for the purpose on the table at which he principally sat.   For additional particulars we are indebted to
the recollections of one of his daughters and to some of
the preserved family letters.   They present De Quincey
to us very touchingly in some of his family relations.
The gentlest of human beings, incapable of a word that
could wound the feelings of any one near him, and indeed
morbidly humble and deferential in his style of address to
persons of every rank, though the uniform ornateness of
his English caused a kind of awe of him among Scottish
servants, he watched his children and moved among them
with a doting attention, in which there was much of the
edifying, while there was nothing of the authoritative.
They grew up in a kind of wondering regard for their
father and his ways, insensibly imbibing refinement from
the little atmosphere of high tastes which, with whatever
appurtenances of disorder and discomfort, his bookish and
studious habits kept around them, and receiving an education of no ordinary kind from his supervision of their
lessons and his discursive fireside talk.   The earliest recollections of the daughter who has been mentioned were
of evenings when, to still her crying in the nursery, her
father would fetch her in his arms into his own warm
room, place her in a chair for the supreme delight of
" sitting up with papa," and, after petting her with sips of
well-sugared coffee, give her a book and paper-cutter with
which to amuse herself while he went on with his writing.
He instructed her, she remembered, even thus early, in

the art of cutting the leaves of books without making
ragged edges. Of his eldest son, William, he was the
sole tutor, bestowing on the task of his education all
that " care and hourly companionship" could do, and with
such effect that the boy could show, at the age of sixteen,
in proof of his scholarship, " not merely an Etonian skill
in the management of Greek metres," but also an original
commentary on Suetonius. Of the opium-eating meanwhile all we know is that, though found indispensable, it
had been, for the most part, brought within bounds.

Three family bereavements fell with heavy effect amid
the occupations and changes of residence of those ten
years. The first was the death by fever, in 1833, of De
Quincey's youngest son, Julius, in the fifth year of his
age. The next was the death, in 1835, at the age of not
quite eighteen, of the above-mentioned eldest son, William,
—" my first-born child, the crown and glory of my life,"
as the poor father wrote afterwards. Then, in 1837, came
the death of the wife and mother herself, the poor Margaret
Simpson from Grasmere, whose lot it had been to marry
this strange man of genius one and twenty years before,
and to accompany him thus far. One can suppose that
hers had not been the easiest or the happiest of lives.
" Delicate health and family cares," says her daughter,
" made her early withdraw from society; but she seems
to have had a powerful fascination for the few friends she
admitted to her intimacy." One of these used to tell the
daughters that he had " never seen a more gracious or a
more beautiful lady "; and it was a standing form of
rebuke to them by an old Scotch charwoman, who had
been much in the house, and continued to usurp some
dominion over them, that none of them would ever be
the brave woman that their mother was. That is all we

know of the dalesman's daughter from Grasmere who died among alien folk in Edinburgh at the age of about thirty-nine, save that they buried her in the West Churchyard, or Churchyard of St. Cuthbert's, beside the children that had gone before her.

There can hardly have been a more helpless widowerhood than that of De Quincey, left in his fifty-second year with six children, the eldest a girl yet in her teens. For two or three years our vision of him and his in their domestic conditions in Edinburgh is an absolute blur, save that we learn that in 1838 he took a lodging for himself at No. 42, Lothian Street, that he might have a separate place for his books and literary labours. But necessity had developed a beautiful power of prudence and self-help among the orphans; and the eldest girl, Margaret, and the next to her in age, Horace, putting their young heads together, struck out a plan. With their father's consent, they took a cottage called Mavis Bush, near Lasswade, about seven miles out of Edinburgh, where they and the four younger ones could live more quietly and economically than in the town, and to which their father could retreat when he wanted retirement. This was in 1840; from which date, on through all the rest of De Quincey's life, the cottage at Lasswade is to be conceived as his chief abode, though without prejudice to the possibility of other refuges and camping-grounds, as the whim occurred to him, in Edinburgh or elsewhere.

# CHAPTER IX.

LASSWADE AND EDINBURGH, WITH VISITS TO GLASGOW: MORE CONTRIBUTIONS TO "BLACKWOOD" AND "TAIT."

1840—1849.

THE name "The Cottage at Lasswade" is somewhat mis-
leading. Lasswade is a village of some extent, reached
most directly from Edinburgh by the road through the
suburb called Newington and thence over the heights of
Liberton and Liberton church, and is situated very prettily
and picturesquely on the river Esk, at a point where that
river has just left the still more picturesque and celebrated
beauties of Hawthornden and the glen of Roslin. But
Mavis Bush Cottage, now styled in the County Directory
"De Quincey Villa," is not in Lasswade, but about a mile
and a half beyond it, near the foot of a bye-road which
descends, by a steep and winding declivity, to that
hollow of the Esk which contains Polton Mills and the
small Polton railway-station. Though too deep-sunk in
the hollow for much cheerfulness of immediate outlook,
it is a snug enough little cottage, with its face direct to
the road and its bit of garden-ground behind, and with a
few other houses about it, above or beneath, on the same
siope. The country round is beautifully hilly, with varied
and pleasant walks, especially pathways by the sides of the
river or up and down its overhanging and well-wooded
banks. The interior of the cottage, when lit up in the

evenings, must have been invitingly cosy in its plain
elegance in the days when it was De Quincey's. " Our
dwelling," he writes to Miss Mitford in 1842, " is a little
" cottage, containing eight rooms only, one of which (the
" largest), on what is called in London the first floor, is
" used as a drawing-room, and one, about half the size, on
" the ground floor, as a dining-room, but for a party of ten
" people at most." He goes on to explain that there were
two servants, and that communication with the post-office
at Lasswade was intermittent and difficult.

For the present we are concerned only with the first
nine years of De Quincey's tenancy of this cottage at
Lasswade or Polton, i.e. with the period between 1840
and 1849, bringing him from his fifty-sixth year to his
sixty-fifth. And, first of all, as has been already stipulated,
the conception of him as located at Lasswade during those
nine years has to be corrected by the fact that he was there
only when he chose. Freak, or the supposed necessities
of his literary work, occasioned pretty frequent removals
from Lasswade to lodgings in Edinburgh and elsewhere.
How many different rooms in various places he thus occupied in the course of the nine years no one has ascertained ;
but, as each in turn was " snowed up " by an accumula-
tion of the books and papers he was using for the time,
and as, in his morbid terror lest these should be lost, it
was usual for him, in leaving any lodging, to entrust the
accumulated deposit to the landlady, he is known to
have had sometimes the rents of " at least four separate
sets of lodgings " all running on simultaneously. It may
be well to collect the particulars of his movements, from
Lasswade and back to it, through the nine years, so far as
the records will serve.

While most of those with whom he had relations were in

H

Edinburgh, there was an attraction also to Glasgow in an
acquaintanceship he had formed with two of the Professors
of Glasgow University. These were Mr. J. P. Nichol,
Professor of Astronomy, a man of fine genius, and the
modest and scholarly Mr. E. L. Lushington, Professor
of Greek. Accordingly, for perhaps the greater part of
the two years from March 1841 to June 1843, De Quincey
was in Glasgow as the guest of one or the other of these
two friends, or in lodgings beside them. His first Glasgow
lodgings were in the High Street, opposite to the Old
College ; but they were exchanged for rooms at 79
Renfield Street. These last were retained and paid for
until as late as 1847. From his return from Glasgow in
June 1843, he seems, with the exception of a plunge now
and then into some unascertainable lodging in Edinburgh,
to have resided steadily at Lasswade. And not without
reason. His eldest son Horace, having gone into the army
as an officer in the 26th Cameronians, had died in China, of
malarious fever, in the end of 1842, after having served in
the Chinese campaign under Sir Hugh Gough ; his third
son, Paul Frederick, had gone out to India as an officer in
the 70th Queen's regiment ; and his second son, Francis,
was in Manchester for the time, as clerk in a commercial
house. The three daughters being thus all of the family
left at Lasswade, De Quincey was bound to be with them
as much as possible. Nothing can be prettier than his
account to Miss Mitford of their life there together and
his description of his daughters. " They live," he says,
" in the most absolute harmony I have ever witnessed.
" Such a sound as that of dissension in any shade or
" degree I have not once heard issuing from their lips.
" And it gladdens me beyond measure that all day long I
" hear from their little drawing-room intermitting sounds

" of gaiety and laughter, the most natural and spontaneous.
" Three sisters more entirely loving to each other, and
" more unaffectedly drawing their daily pleasures from
" sources that will always continue to lie in their power,
" viz. books and music, I have not either known or heard
" of." So through 1844, 1845, and 1846, but with the
variation caused in the household by the return, in 1845,
of the son Francis from Manchester, to exchange his
prospects in commerce for the study of Medicine at the
University of Edinburgh. The exchange was not without
its difficulties, for the young man had to walk from Lasswade to Edinburgh every day to attend the classes ; but it
gave De Quincey the pleasant additional occupation of
inquiring into his son's progress and coaching him for some
of his examinations. Then there were pleasant acquain-
tanceships with some of the Lasswade neighbours, with
drives now and then of the father and daughters to town
together, and the still more frequent reception of friends
and admirers of De Quincey who made their way to
Lasswade to pay him their respects. In 1847 there was
another long absence in Glasgow, extending from January
to October. During part of the time his daughters were
on a visit, the first in their lives, to their father's surviving
relatives in the West of England ; and some letters of
his show a lively interest in their reported movements
amid the scenes and persons that had been so familiar to
himself in his earlier days, and a special pleasure in the
fact that they had met Mr. Walter Savage Landor.
Through 1848 and 1849 all the family were together again
at Lasswade, with no other break in the routine there than
might be caused by De Quincey's incurable passion for
hiding himself at his option now and then in some
Edinburgh lodging.

An important matter all this while, as in every preceding period of De Quincey's existence, had been the state of his health. It may be doubted whether the majority of those interested in him have had any adequate conception of that extreme fragility of body, that complexity of bodily pains and ailments, with which, even apart from the opium, he had to contend all his life. Connected with his main malady,—that malady into which all his inherited or acquired ailments had coalesced and settled from an early stage of his youth, and which the medical authorities are disposed to define as "gastrodynia" or severe gastric neuralgia, accompanied by "a low inflammatory condition of the mucous coat of the stomach, proceeding at times to ulceration,"—there was a specific inability to live by the ordinary forms of nutriment. His teeth had gone; he "did not know what it was to eat a dinner"; his message in 1847 to an old schoolfellow, by way of jocular apology for never having renewed their old acquaintance by letter, was that he had not once dined "since shaking hands with him in the eighteenth century." A little soup, tea, cocoa, coffee, or other fluid, with a sop of bread, or more rarely an inch or two of mutton or hare, kept to the extreme of tenderness, and cut finically for easy mastication, formed De Quincey's diet. In the management even of this there was incessant cause of nervous irritation. Add the glooms and phrenzies growing out of the indulgence in opium to which he had so long been habituated. In this matter there had been ups and downs within our present period, according to the varying degrees of his suffering from his independent malady, but also according to the fluctuations of his reasonings for and against the drug. The chief crisis, marked as such by De Quincey himself in a kind of diary of notes and jottings at the time, had been in the year 1844. In some new access of accumulated wretchedness, mental and physical, when a horror of the most hideous blackness seemed once more to be "travelling over the disc of his life," he had rioted again with the fiend and exulted in 5000 daily drops of the liquid damnation. The rebound towards self-retrieval, as it is chronicled in his jottings, had cost him efforts incredible. He had experimented in reductions of the dose and even in the torture of total abstinence; and, his feet having failed him for his ordinary pedestrian exercise in the roads between Lasswade and Edinburgh, he had compelled himself to shuffle round and round the garden of his Lasswade cottage in a measured circuit of forty-four yards, so as to accomplish in that way his ten miles a day. Unexpectedly, these efforts had succeeded; and, with an allowance ranging from 100 drops a day upwards, he had recovered in 1844 the faculty of living on. In 1848 there had been another crisis, but less formidable; and from that date, we are given to understand, his wrestlings with opium were at an end. Having ascertained the very minimum of the drug on which existence was endurable in his own case, he kept to that as much as possible through the rest of his life, and saw no use in troubling himself with further experimentation.

De Quincey's literary labours during the nine years had still been chiefly in contributions to *Blackwood* and *Tait*. To *Blackwood* his chief contributions had been as follows:—In 1841, *The Secret Societies of Asia, Plato's Republic, Traits and Tendencies of German Literature* (?), *Homer and the Homeridæ* (three parts); in 1842, *Philosophy of Herodotus, The Pagan Oracles, Cicero, Ricardo made Easy* (three parts), *Benjamin of Tudela* (?); in

1844, *Greece under the Romans;* in 1845, *Coleridge and Opium-Eating,* and *Suspiria de Profundis, being a Sequel to the Confessions of an Opium-Eater* (three successive articles, with sub-titles) ; and, in 1849, *The English Mail-Coach,* and *The Vision of Sudden Death.* To *Tait* there seem to have been no contributions between 1841 and 1845 ; but in this latter year the series in that magazine was renewed in an article on *Wordsworth's Poetry,* followed by another *On the Temperance Movement,* and by several papers under the general title of *Notes on Gil-fillan's Gallery of Literary Portraits.* These last, treating of Godwin, Hazlitt, Shelley, Keats, &c., were continued into 1846,—in which year also appeared two papers on *The Antigone of Sophocles,* occasioned by a dramatic performance at Edinburgh by Miss Helen Faucit, two on *Christianity considered as an Organ of Political Movement,* one entitled *Glance at the Works of Mackintosh,* and one entitled *System of the Heavens as revealed by Lord Rosse's Telescope.* To these succeeded, in 1847, *Notes on Walter Savage Landor, Joan of Arc* (two papers), *Schlosser's Literary History of the Eighteenth Century, Milton versus Southey and Landor, Orthographic Mutineers, The Spanish Military Nun* (three papers), and two papers on *Protestantism,* completed by a third in February 1848. When we add that De Quincey had some connexion during a portion of the nine years with a Glasgow newspaper, and that his *Logic of Political Economy* (now included in his Collected Works) was first published in separate book-form by Messrs. Blackwood in 1844, it will be seen that his literary industry through the period had continued very vigorous indeed. Through the greater part of the nine years the chief stimulus, as before, had been actual need of money ; but, towards the end of the period there had been a considerable abatement of the urgency of this particular motive by the falling-in of legacies from his uncle, his mother, or other relatives. Particulars are not given ; but one infers, from hints in the published family letters, that the year 1847 was a marked turning-point of relief for the brain-worn veteran in this respect.

The brain-worn veteran ! The phrase does not imply that there were yet any signs in him of mental decrepitude. On the contrary, as the titles of some of the articles in the last paragraph will have suggested, the sexagenarian De Quincey was still in the full perfection of his wonderful powers. Whatever might have been the case seventeen years before, when he first settled permanently in Edinburgh, it would have been no wonder now if the community of that city had learnt to think of him as one of the few worthiest among them *digito monstrari* as he passed in their streets. It had not come quite to that length in De Quincey's case,—the peculiar nature of his celebrity not making him liable to any such rush of popular and day-light recognition as gathered round Wilson or Chalmers, but coupling him rather with such a similar recluse and late burner of the lamp as the philosophic Hamilton. Still, for all in Edinburgh who had any special passion for literature, or thought they had, De Quincey from 1845 onwards was most emphatically one of the " characters " of the place. He was talked of and gossiped about at dinner-tables and tea-tables, and to see him, even by stratagem, was worth an effort. As it was the chance of the present writer to be in the vicinity for a part of the precise time mentioned (from

December 1844 to May 1847), he will here set down, as
authentically as he can, first what he then heard, and
next what trifle he saw, of the little local wonder.

The rumours about De Quincey were invariably to the
effect that his eccentricity, his difference from other
mortals, passed all bounds of belief or conception. The form
of his eccentricity generally reported first was the absolute
uncertainty of his whereabouts at that particular time,
arising from his evasiveness on the subject of his lodgings
when he was last seen, or intimation from him that, having
changed his lodgings, he was in the distressing predicament
of having an adversary in pursuit of him in the shape of
a former landlady.   This suspiciousness of being pursued
had become an ingrained habit of De Quincey's mind, and
accounted for much of his conduct.   It connected itself
with his astounding incompetence in money-matters.   In
that department of practice the abstract political economist, so profound in Ricardo, was helpless as an infant.
He gave away money right and left when he had it, and
was then the prince of almoners for sorners and beggars ;
but he was constantly running aground himself.   The
reports of him in this respect agreed pretty uniformly in
the idea that his difficulties did not necessarily arise from
want of money, but only, or often, from want of a particular sum required at a particular moment and inability in
all ordinary processes for converting the potential into the
actual.   Mr. Hill Burton gives an Edinburgh illustration
of about our present date which reminds one of Mr.
Charles Knight's story of the bank-draft in London in the
year 1825.   One night very late, he tells us, De Quincey,
arriving at a friend's door, and having obtained admission
with difficulty, explained, with all the skill and pathos of
his beautiful rhetoric, that it was absolutely essential he

should be provided at once with 7s. 6d.  On perceiving
surprise on his friend's face, he proceeded to explain that
he had a document in his possession the transference of
which to his friend's care would probably obviate his
hesitation ; and then, after rummaging in his pockets, and
fetching a miscellany of small articles out of them, he
produced at last a crumpled piece of paper, which he
tendered as security.   It was a 50l. note ; and his friend's
impression was that, if he had kept the note in exchange
for the 7s. 6d., he would have heard no more of the
transaction, and indeed that, before coming to his door,
De Quincey had been trying to negotiate the exchange at
a series of shops, and had failed only through extreme
scepticism on the part of the shopkeepers.   From these
reports of the mysteriousness of De Quincey's usual whereabouts, and his tendency to come to light only occasionally
in the straits of some dilemma, it was a natural inference
that a meeting with him in any ordinary social way was not
a matter of easy arrangement.   A promise from him, you
were told, was of no use : the party might meet, expecting
him ; but, ten to one, De Quincey would not be there.
There was, however, a science of the ways and means of
getting at De Quincey ; in which science, according to
experts, the method of surest efficacy was to commission
some one to find him out and bring him.   Then, if pre-
caution made escape impossible, he would come meekly
and unresistingly.   But in what guise would he come ?
What a question for endless speculation this was may be
guessed from Mr. Hill Burton's account of his appearance
at one important dinner-party, to which he had been lured
by such deep-laid pretences that he came without convoy.
" The festivities of the afternoon are far on when a
" commotion is heard in the hall as if some dog or other

" stray animal had forced his way in. The instinct of a
" friendly guest tells him of the arrival : he opens the door
" and fetches in the little stranger. What can it be ? A
" street-boy of some sort ? His costume, in fact, is a boy's
" duffle great-coat, very threadbare, with a hole in it,
" and buttoned tight to the chin, where it meets the
" fragments of a particoloured belcher handkerchief; on
" his feet are list shoes, covered with snow, for it is a
" stormy winter-night ; and the trousers !—some one sug-
" gests that they are mere linen garments blackened with
" writing-ink, but that Papaverius never would have been
" at the trouble so to disguise them. What can be the
" theory of such a costume ? The simplest thing in the
" world,—it consisted of the fragments of apparel nearest
" at hand. Had chance thrown to him a court single-
" breasted coat, with a bishop's apron, a kilt, and top-
" boots, in these he would have made his entry." Dressed
in whatever fashion, he was still De Quincey, and you
were glad to have him. For as to the magic of his talk,
its sweet and subtle ripple of anecdote and suggestion, its
witching splendour when he rose to his highest, the reports
were unanimous and enthusiastic. No conceivable intellectual treat, you were told, was equal to a fortunate evening
with De Quincey. Only, you were pretty sure to hear,
there might be one drawback. Whether from the stimulus
of opium or not, he was apt to be at his best when it was
rapidly becoming to-morrow and his companions had to
think of going. Having got your De Quincey, you might
thus find yourself face to face with the problem how to get
rid of him. Generally it solved itself by his going at last
with the rest, steering himself no one knew whither
through the starlight or darkness ; but sometimes, you
were told, on polite inducement, he would remain where

he was, and then the visit of an evening might extend
itself to unknown dimensions.

Such were the reports one heard about De Quincey
before seeing him.  My own few glimpses of him, I am
bound to add, did not present him to me in any such
extreme of helplessness as the reports had prepared me to
expect.  Here are the facts, as I have already printed
them elsewhere : — " The first time I saw De Quincey was
" most pleasantly one evening in a room high up in one
" of the tall houses of the Old Town.  He came in charge
" of a strong, determined man, who took all the necessary
" trouble.  There were but few present, and all went on
" nicely.  In addition to the general impression of
" diminutiveness and fragility, one was struck with the
" peculiar beauty of his head and forehead, rising dis-
" proportionately high over his small wrinkly visage and
" gentle deep-set eyes.  In his talk, which was in the
" form of really harmonious and considerate colloquy, and
" not at all in that of monologue, I remember chiefly two
" incidents.  The birthday of some one present having been
" mentioned, De Quincey immediately said ' O, that is the
" anniversary of the battle of So-and-So' ; and he seemed
" ready to catch as many birthdays as might be thrown
" him on the spot, and almanack them all round in a
" similar manner from his memory.  The other incident
" was his use of a phrase very beautiful in itself, and
" which seemed characteristic of his manner of thinking.
" Describing some visionary scene or other, he spoke of it
" as consisting of ' discs of light and interspaces of gloom' ;
" and I noticed that, with all the fine distinctness of the
" phrase, both optical and musical, it came from him with
" no sort of consciousness of its being out of the way in
" talk, and with no reference whatever to its being

" appreciated or not by those around him, but simply
" because, whoever might be listening, he would be thinking
" as De Quincey. That evening passed ; and, though I
" saw him once or twice again, it is the last sight of him
" that I remember next best. It must have been, I think,
" in 1846, on a summer afternoon. A friend, a stranger
" in Edinburgh, was walking with me in one of the
" pleasant, quiet country lanes near the town. Meeting
" us, and the sole moving thing in the lane besides our-
" selves, came a small figure, not untidily dressed, but with
" his hat pushed up far in front over his forehead, and
" hanging on his hind-head, so that the back rim must
" have been resting on his coat-collar. At a little distance
" I recognised it to be De Quincey ; but, not considering
" myself entitled to interrupt his meditations, I only
" whispered the information to my friend, that he might
" not miss what the look at such a celebrity was worth.
" So we passed him, giving him the wall. Not un-
" naturally, however, after he passed, we turned round for
" the pleasure of a back view of the wee intellectual
" wizard. Whether my whisper and our glances had
" alarmed him, as a ticket-of-leave man might be rendered
" uneasy in his solitary walk by the scrutiny of two passing
" strangers, or whether he had some recollection of me
" (which was likely enough, as he seemed to forget no-
" thing), I do not know ; but we found that he too had
" stopped and was looking round at us. Apparently
" scared at being caught doing so, he immediately wheeled
" round again, and hurried his pace towards a side-turning
" from the lane, into which he disappeared, his hat still
" hanging on the back of his head. That was my last
" sight of De Quincey."

Those walks of De Quincey in the environs of Edin-

burgh ought to linger still among the memories of the
legend-loving town. The particular walk just mentioned
was in daylight, and the meeting was in the quiet lane or
road by which, avoiding the great Dean Road, one wends
towards the Corstorphines and Craigcrook. Jeffrey was
then alive, and resident at Craigcrook ; but it is quite impossible that De Quincey had been calling on Jeffrey.
His walks were in all directions, for his own purposes of
exercise or recreation only, and at his own sweet will.
By preference also, and in the proportion of many to one,
the longest of them were nocturnal. It is strange yet to
think of the little figure in those weary wanderings of his
round and through the city evening after evening, now on
his way from Lasswade inwards over the darkening heights
and hollows to the Old Town, now along the glittering
chasm of Princes Street or the gloomier regularity of George
Street, now down by the northern suburbs to the levels
of the Firth at Granton, now by a daring meander east-
wards to the deserted ghastliness of Leith Pier and the
skeleton array of masts and shipping, and always, or often,
with the penance of the returning zigzag somehow to
Lasswade and the cottage on the Esk. It was his custom,
we are told, in these nocturnal rambles, and chiefly for his
convenience in certain intricate labyrinths of pathway
about the Esk, with a foot-bridge or two in them, to carry
a small lantern, with the means of lighting it when he
chose. What a trial to the nerves of the hardiest belated
tramp, or other night-bird, with any dread of the supernatural, to have come upon De Quincey in such a spot,
striking his match by a bush, or advancing through the
trees with his bull's-eye ! He himself was perfectly fear-
less of night-bird or demon. Night was his natural
element ; what could it bring forth that should alarm

*him ?* Sometimes, we are informed, though without production of the evidence, he would not care to return home
at all, but would lie down for rest and shelter anywhere.
Edinburgh, therefore, in preserving her legends about the
De Quincey who honoured her with so much of his life, has
to remember, it seems, unless rumour has been too inventive, that not only were his footsteps familiar with every
mile of road round her, but sometimes he would bivouac
in a wayside wood in her neighbourhood, or on a spur of
the Braids or the Pentlands, canopied only by the con-
stellations.

The danger is that, in dwelling so much on the eccentricities of De Quincey, it should be forgotten that all the
while the cottage at Lasswade was really his home. It
was there that he would have been detained always by
those dearest to him; and it was there, in fact, with all
allowance for his wanderings and fugitations, that he did
spend most of his time. Very soon, if left to himself, he
would have taken possession of every room in the house,
one after another, and "snowed up" each with his papers;
but, that having been gently prevented, he had one room to
work in all day and all night to his heart's content. The
evenings, or the intervals between his daily working-time
and his nightly working-time or stroll, he generally
spent in the drawing-room with his daughters, either
alone or in company with any friends that chanced
to be with them. At such times, we are told, he was
unusually charming. "The newspaper was brought out,
" and he, telling in his own delightful way, rather than
" reading, the news, would, on questions from this one or
" that one of the party, often including young friends of
" his children, neighbours, or visitors from distant places,
" illuminate the subject with such a wealth of memories,

" of old stories, of past or present experiences, of humour,
" of suggestion, even of prophecy, as by its very wealth
" makes it impossible to give any taste of it." The
description is by one of his daughters ; and she adds a
touch which is inimitable in its fidelity and tenderness.
" He was not," she says, " a reassuring man for nervous
" people to live with, as those nights were exceptions on
" which he did not set something on fire, the commonest
" incident being for some one to look up from book or
" work to say casually, *Papa, your hair is on fire ;* of
" which a calm *Is it, my love ?* and a hand rubbing out
" the blaze was all the notice taken." The music, which
was so frequently a part of those indoor pleasures, and the
variations of the character of the evenings now and then
by the presence of distinguished visitors, British or
American, may easily be imagined. What has chiefly to
be borne in mind, we repeat, is that, at the centre of all
De Quincey's Bohemian roamings, real and reputed, there
was this home of warmth and comfort for him on the
banks of the Esk, and that it may be seen by those who
feel an interest in him to this day. The quickest way is
to take the rail from Edinburgh to the Polton station ; but
the best is to go to Lasswade, and thence to walk the mile
and a half extra that bring one to the spot.

# CHAPTER X.

LASSWADE, AND NO. 42 LOTHIAN STREET, EDINBURGH :
THE COLLECTED WORKS : LAST DAYS OF DE QUINCEY.

1849—1859.

In 1845 there had been started, by Mr. James Hogg,
an enterprising Edinburgh bookseller, a new cheap periodical, called *Hogg's Weekly Instructor*. The periodical
had been going on for three years, and had entered on a
" new series" in 1848. It was in the autumn of 1849,
when some accident had caused the removal of the print-
ing-offices to temporary premises in the suburb of Edinburgh called Canonmills, that Mr. Hogg, attending to some
matters there, was told that a stranger wanted to speak to
him. " Going down," says Mr. Hogg, " I was confronted
" by a noticeably small figure, attired in a capacious gar-
" ment, which was much too large, and which served the
" purpose of both undercoat and overcoat." It was, in
fact, De Quincey, who had come to offer an article for
the *Instructor*. Mr. Hogg, having ascertained who his
visitor was, very naturally accepted the article at once ;
whereupon it was produced from an inner pocket of the
capacious great-coat, and handed to Mr. Hogg, but not till
De Quincey had produced from the same pocket a small
handbrush and carefully brushed the manuscript. Finding
he had come all the way from Lasswade, Mr. Hogg asked
him how he was to get back. He would walk, as usual,

he said.  It was now about six o'clock, and he would be
home before nine.

This call on Mr. Hogg at Canonmills turned out of no
small importance in De Quincey's biography.  Whether
it had been occasioned by any knowledge on De Quincey's
part that his connexion with *Blackwood* and *Tait* was
coming to an end, or merely by a wish to have a weekly
periodical also at hand for the reception of smaller odds
and ends from his pen, certain it is that from 1849 the
new connexion all but superseded every other.  There are
no known contributions by De Quincey to *Blackwood*
after 1849; his only known contribution to *Tait* after
that date was a paper in three instalments, in 1851, entitled *Lord Carlisle on Pope ;* and, though *The North
British Review* is said to have counted De Quincey
among its contributors, his literary exertions in any such
quarter were but asides from his occupations for Mr.
Hogg.  Not, of course, that these occupations consisted in
mere contributorship to *Hogg's Instructor.*  That periodical, whether under its original name, which it retained
till 1856, or under the more appalling name of TITAN,
which it adopted in 1857, did indeed receive bright occasional contributions from De Quincey.  The most notable
were a short sketch of *Professor Wilson* in 1850, an
article on *Sir William Hamilton* in three portions in
1852, a paper on *California* in 1852, and one on *China*
in 1857.  But what were a few stray articles in an Edinburgh weekly for the last ten years of such a life as De
Quincey's ?  How had it come to pass, in fact, that a
man for whose articles all editors and all publishers in the
British Islands, had they been really deep in their craft,
ought to have been competing, had found it necessary, in
his sixty-fifth year, to pay that call at Canonmills with a

I

manuscript in his pocket, and solicit, almost as a mendicant, the acceptance of it for the columns of a struggling Edinburgh weekly? That mystery resolves itself into the more general mystery of the origin of stupidity; but the call at Canonmills had at least one result more fortunate than the opening for De Quincey of another small source of wages by periodical-writing in his old age. Mr. Hogg, having to see his new contributor again and again, conceived a possible expansion of their connexion. Why should he not bring out, under De Quincey's own editorial supervision, a collective edition of De Quincey's Works? True, it had been announced that the scheme had been already entertained in some quarters and given up as hopeless; true, it was the uniform representation to Mr. Hogg by his brothers in business that, if he did begin the enterprise with De Quincey's consent, it would break down after a volume or two, through De Quincey's unpunctuality and incapacity for continuous labour. "I will risk it," said Mr. Hogg to himself; and he did. It seems to have been in 1850 that the resolution was taken, though the preparations were not begun till some time later.

Meanwhile the same idea had occurred to the American publishing firm of Messrs. Ticknor and Fields of Boston. In America, almost always in advance of the mother-country in such matters, it had been perceived long ago that De Quincey was one of the chief English Classics. There had been popular American reprints already of individual pieces of his; and it was Mr. Fields himself that now undertook the task of seeking out his scattered articles in British periodicals and collecting and arranging them in proper form. For this first American edition of De Quincey's works, begun in 1851, and completed in 1855 in twenty volumes, the publishers obtained some assistance from De Quincey while it was in progress; and it is remembered to their credit that they made him a participator in the profits to a handsome extent. The Boston edition of the works, however, was not to interfere with Mr. Hogg's projected Edinburgh edition; which, indeed, was to differ from the Boston edition very considerably. Less complete in some respects, inasmuch as De Quincey was to omit from it articles that are kept in the Boston edition, and was to diminish the bulk of the matter on certain subjects by fusing separate articles in some cases into one, it was, on the other hand, to be more perfect, in so far as it was to receive the author's own revision throughout, with modifications and extensions in the course of the revision.

To get rid of that matter at once, it may be stated that, when the first volume of the Edinburgh edition did appear in 1853, it appeared as the first volume of a series the general title of which was to be *Selections Grave and Gay, from writings published and unpublished, by Thomas De Quincey*, and that this general title was maintained till the issue of the fourteenth volume of the series (the last to which it was carried by Mr. Hogg) in 1860. On the whole, it is to be regretted now that De Quincey did not, for this edition, simply collect his writings, and publish them in the chronological order of their first appearance or their composition, with a note of date and place to each. Next best would have been an assortment of the papers into sets of volumes according to a classification of their subjects. No one was more capable of such a classification than De Quincey; but, unfortunately, he had no complete preserved collection of his printed papers by him, or of the periodicals containing them. The American edition, coming over to him in suc-

cessive volumes, was his greatest help; but, till it was
complete, and sometimes even then, he had to rummage
for his old papers, or employ Mr. Hogg to rummage for
him, hurriedly squeezing together what was readiest at
intervals, to make up a volume when the press became
ravenous. Hence the most provoking jumble in the contents of the fourteen volumes,—mixed kinds of matter in
the same volume, and dispersion of the same kinds of
matter over volumes wide apart, and yet all with a pre-
tence of grouping and with factitious sub-titles invented
for the separate volumes on the spur of the moment.
Much of this has been remedied in the later issues of the
same Edinburgh edition by Messrs. A. and C. Black, who
acquired the property in 1862. Two volumes have been
added by Messrs. Black to the previous fourteen, and
other alterations have been made by them, justifying the
exchange of the title *Selections Grave and Gay*, &c., for
the more comprehensive title *De Quincey's Works*.

The new labour of bringing out the Collected Works
occasioned a change in De Quincey's domiciliary arrangements. It may be remembered that from 1838 to 1840,
or just after his wife's death and before the happy notion
of the cottage at Lasswade, his Edinburgh lodging or
working headquarters had been at No. 42 Lothian Street.
There seems reason for believing that, though he had
been in a variety of lodging-places in the interval, he had
always preferred this. At all events, in 1852, when
he was in the throes of the first volume of the
Collected Works, there was a return to No. 42 Lothian
Street, and this time, as it turned out, for so permanent a
tenancy that no house in Edinburgh now can compete
with that in the interest of its associations with De
Quincey.

Lothian Street, the stranger to Edinburgh may be informed, is a dense street of shops and rather dingy
houses, in the Old Town, close to the University; and
No. 42, like most of the other houses, is what is called
in Edinburgh "a common stair." In other words, it is a
tenement entered from the street by an arched passage,
from which a stone staircase ascends to the several half-
flats into which the whole is divided, each with its independent door and door-bell. There are six such half-
flats above the ground-floor; and that in which De
Quincey had his rooms was the left half-flat on the second
floor. The half-flat was then, as it had been at the time
of De Quincey's first familiarity with it, in the occupation
of a widowed Mrs. Wilson and her sister Miss Stark.
They were two most worthy persons, who had come to
have some appreciation of the extraordinary character of
their lodger; and they were from this time forward to
take the most exemplary charge of him. It is an additional satisfaction to know that, soon after they had taken
charge of him, and chiefly by Mr. Hogg's friendly exertions, he was disentangled from all his supposed perplexi-
ties with other landladies and lodging-house keepers.
Mr. Hogg's statements on this point, a vital one in De
Quincey's biography, are worth remembering.—Having,
with some difficulty, obtained the necessary information
from him, and permission to act in his name, Mr. Hogg
did find that deposits of papers had been left by him in
various places. In the main, however, he found that De
Quincey's dread that he could be pursued on account of
claims so arising was a mere hallucination. Two former
landladies came of their own accord, and with perfect
good nature, to deliver up to Mr. Hogg, without any
claim whatever, papers of the strange little gentleman

who had lodged with them; in a third case, where a
claim for house-room was presented, which troubled De
Quincey for some time, it was so clearly exorbitant that
it might have been quashed at once but for De Quincey's
anxiety about the safety of his papers; and the most
flagrant case of all was one in which a whole family
trafficked on their possession of papers of De Quincey's as
a means of extorting money from him, though not pro-
fessing that he owed them a farthing. They played on
his fears for his papers, doling them out in parcels, and
sometimes sending him "bogus-packets," made up of
anything; they pleaded abject poverty, and appealed to
his pity; and at least once they got up a death in the
family, that he might have the pleasure of contributing to
the funeral expenses. The note sent to De Quincey on
this occasion, and forwarded by him to Mr. Hogg, is a
curiosity. "Mr. De Quincey, sir," it begins, "in accord-
"ance with your request, I have made out the enclosed
"items, money for which I would want for my mother's
"funeral. She is to be buried to-morrow, and would like
"things settled as early as possible to-day." Mr. Hogg
having taken the wretches in hand, they were brought
under some sort of control; but there is a trace of trouble
from them to as late as 1855.—Two more of Mr. Hogg's
stories about De Quincey relate to the same matter of his
ubiquitously-scattered papers. Once, in a hotel in the
High Street, into which he had taken De Quincey for refuge and a basin of soup during a thunder-shower, the
waiter, after looking at De Quincey, said "I think, sir, I
have a bundle of papers which you left here some time
ago"; and, sure enough, a bundle was produced, which
De Quincey had left there about a year before. Another
time, having gone to Glasgow once more on a visit to

Professor Lushington, and having taken two tea-chests of papers with him, he had been obliged, by some refractoriness on the part of the porter, to leave them at a bookseller's shop on their way to the Professor's house. This he remembered perfectly ; but, as he had taken no note of the name of the bookseller, or the number of the shop, or even of the name of the street, Mr. Hogg found him quite rueful on the subject after his return to Edinburgh. A letter to a friend and a round of inquiries among the Glasgow booksellers made all right ; and Mr. Hogg had the pleasure of pointing out to him the two recovered boxes as they lay in his office, and asking what was to be done with them. "Send them to Lothian Street," was the answer ; and thither they were accordingly sent, an addition to the vast aggregate of books, periodicals, and newspapers, in mounds on the floor and in tiers along the walls, already crammed into his rooms, and vexing the orderly souls of Mrs. Wilson and Miss Stark.

A worrying, and yet most amusing, business it was for Mr. Hogg to keep De Quincey, in those rooms, or in his occasional adjournments to Lasswade, to his great task of bringing out, with due punctuality, the successive volumes of his Collected Works. It was one long struggle between De Quincey and the printing-press. A message-boy, named Roderick, was kept always ready at the one end, to be shot to Lothian Street or Lasswade for copy when the supply failed ; at the other end was De Quincey himself, groaning and working. His preserved notes to Mr. Hogg, excusing his failures and delays, are pathetically characteristic. "My non-performances after circumstantial notice have "been so many," he says in one, "that I can hardly hope "for any credit when I tell you that on Monday I shall "be in Lothian Street with the MS. all ready for the

" press." The excuse on this occasion was his " nervous
sufferings "; but another time it is trouble about some
unpaid taxes, and consequent "agitation at the prospect of
utter ruin past all repair." Again, it is uncertainty
whether certain papers are already in the printer's hands
or are still in his own possession, with a desire to be sure
on the point, so as to be saved, if possible, " a process of
stooping " in search of them, from which he could " hardly
recover for a fortnight." Once it is owing to "lumbago";
once to his having fallen asleep inopportunely ; another
time to partial delirium from " want of sleep and opium
combined "; another time, to distraction from " having
been up and writing all night," with the addition " I have
just set fire to my hair." Once the delay is due to "a
process of whitewashing or otherwise cleaning ceilings,
&c.," which has been going on in the house, and to the
unfortunate fact that most of the papers needed at the
moment " had been placed within a set of drawers against
which is now reared the whitewasher's scaffolding "; and
several times it is owing to consideration for Miss Stark,
who is not in the best of health, and has too much to do.
Miss Stark, in fact, had become indispensable to him, not
only buying for him all the articles he wanted, articles of
apparel included, but also receiving and returning messages
for him, and sorting and numbering his slips of copy, and
so minutely cognisant of his daily dealings and difficulties
with the press that she began to fancy she was herself a
kind of literary lady.[1] It is curious to observe, amid all

[1] Miss Stark is still alive, and in the same No. 42 Lothian
Street ; and I have had the pleasure of seeing her, and hearing her
talk of De Quincey, in the very rooms which he occupied. She
remembers that he usually wrote on papers which he held in his
left hand, near his eyes, and not at a table, and also that he had

this confusion, the indefatigable and painstaking laborious-
ness of the little workman, his fastidious care for accuracy,
and his delicate regard for the feelings and interests of
other people.   His notes of excuse are themselves models
of superfluous precision; and his instructions to the
compositors for corrections of the press and for the proper
reading of his manuscript are elaborately over-cautious.
He is unhappy sometimes at the thought that the
compositors, whose time is their fortune, may be standing
idle through his fault; and once he is miserable till he
has explained to Mr. Hogg by two letters in succession
that the boy Roderick is not to blame for a certain mis-
understanding, but had delivered his message with Spartan
strictness.   Nor, in the long-run, as Mr. Hogg vouches,
did De Quincey fail in any essential of his undertaking.
In the accounts between them he was equally scrupulous,
and indeed morbidly afraid of any benefit to himself by a
casual error.   It was not long before Mr. Hogg found that
a cheque made him uneasy, and that he would always
rather have a little cash on account..   From another source
we learn that he did not like the greasy Scotch one-pound
notes, but preferred the medallions of her Majesty's head
in gold, silver, or copper.

While No. 42 Lothian Street was De Quincey's
established abode and workshop from 1852 onwards, it
was at Lasswade, as before, that he was mainly or solely
to be seen by visitors.   The domestic economy there, however, did not remain unchanged.   In 1853 there was the
first break in the household by the marriage of his eldest

a peculiar way of notching each slip of manuscript when he had
done with it.   He had a secret meaning in the practice, which he
promised to tell her; but he never did.   She does not remember
that he went out much at nights, or indeed during the day, except
for transit to Lasswade.

daughter, Margaret, to Mr. Robert Craig, the son of a
highly-respected neighbour, and the removal of the married
pair to Ireland. In 1854 the two younger daughters were
away from Lasswade for some time, on a visit to their
married sister in her new home ; and in 1855 the elder of
these, Florence, went out to India, to become the wife of
Colonel Baird Smith, an engineer officer of high distinction, whose name and services are still brilliant in our
Indian annals. As by that time the medical son Francis
had become a duly-qualified physician and gone out to
Brazil, De Quincey seems to have felt some compunction
afterwards in leaving his single remaining daughter,
Emily, so much alone at Lasswade. There were pathetic
signs of this, Mrs. Baird Smith informs us, in the increased frequency thenceforward of his affectionate notes
and letters from Lothian Street to Lasswade when he
could not come himself ; and her explanation of the whole
matter is :—" He really could not manage his work farther
" from the press, and nothing which would have been
" natural in other cases, such as my sister's removing into
" Edinburgh, would have answered with him." Indeed,
though Miss De Quincey's most natural home was still the
pretty place on the Esk to which she had been accustomed
from her childhood, and where, rather than in Edinburgh,
she had pleasant neighbourly ties, she was inevitably
absent from it a good deal, after 1855, on visits elsewhere,
more especially to her sister, Mrs. Craig, in Ireland. In
one such visit, in the autumn of 1857, De Quincey himself
actually accompanied her,—the arrival just then of his
youngest son, Paul Frederick, on furlough from his
regiment in India, having suggested the journey and made
the travelling arrangements easier. Even with such an
escort, it was something of an adventure for De Quincey

in his seventy-third year; but all was managed to his mind; and there was a new fund of delight for him through the rest of his life in the fact that he had made out this visit to his eldest daughter in her Irish home, and had *seen* the two little ones that were to remember him as their grandfather. From that date there was to be no similar interruption of his usual habits, but only, whenever his youngest daughter was at Lasswade, the customary alternation between the familiar cottage there and his own crib in Lothian Street. Even after he had passed his seventieth year he retained so much of his pedestrian vigour that the distance of seven miles between the two places was nothing to him if he were in the humour, and younger men were surprised at the ease with which he preceded them up one of the braes of the Esk. Latterly, however, there was an increasing feebleness, bringing his rambles more and more within bounds, and sometimes confining him to his Lothian Street rooms for weeks together. A tendency to somnambulism, which showed itself now and then, was a new cause of trepidation on his account to Mrs. Wilson and Miss Stark, already sufficiently in dread of nightly accident to him and his papers from his extreme shortsightedness and perpetual contact with fire and lighted candles. On the other hand, one is glad to find, he was in his latter years comparatively free from the pains and miseries of his constitutional malady. The testimony to this fact is concurrent from several quarters; and the medical hypothesis now is that the "lesion of the stomach" which had been the prime cause of his sufferings, and the explanation of his abnormal consumption of opium, had somehow begun to heal itself, by a kind of natural induration, as old age came on.

The De Quincey of the ten years from 1849 to 1859,

the De Quincey whose voluminous Collected Works were appearing simultaneously in a British edition and an American edition, was naturally an object of even keener social curiosity than the De Quincey of earlier and less rounded-off celebrity. He was thought of as a surviving chief of a former generation, whom one must make haste to see, if he were ever to be seen at all. For the Edinburgh people generally, however, to see De Quincey was no more easy matter now than it had been before. His elusiveness of all ordinary social gatherings had increased rather than diminished; and from that network of great dinner-parties and great evening assemblies which brings all Edinburgh together, over and over again, every season from November to May, he was still allowed to escape by a unanimous vote in favour of his intractable singularity. So long as Wilson lived, it was never the fault of that heartiest and most hospitable of men if he lost sight of De Quincey for any considerable while, or were not applied to first for any act of friendship, or of guardianship in a difficulty, that De Quincey might need. But Wilson died in April, 1854, at the age of sixty-nine, leaving his weaker-bodied friend, then of the same age, to live on for nearly six years more of lingering Edinburgh independence. Among friends of De Quincey's who saw most of him in his later years, before Wilson's death or after, were Mr. Robert Chambers, Mr. Hill Burton, Mr. Alexander Russel of the *Scotsman*, and Mr. J. R. Findlay. Those were still the days too of the pleasant little supper-parties of Mrs. Crowe in Darnaway Street, remembered yet by some, and certainly by the present writer, as among the most excellent and best-managed things of the kind ever known in Edinburgh or elsewhere. By the kindly tact of the hostess, one was always sure to meet at her table, in the

easiest and friendliest fashion, from half-a-dozen to ten or
twelve of the men and women best worth knowing, on
literary or other grounds, among the residents in Edinburgh or the last week's arrivals.  As I write, there rise
up in my memory the genial old Sir William Allan and
his niece, Mr. and Mrs. George Combe (the latter a
daughter of Mrs. Siddons, and with a flash of her mother's
dramatic power in her at unexpected moments), the good
Robert Chambers, Dr. Samuel Brown, David Scott, Miss
Rigby, Mrs. Stirling of Hill Street, the American Miss
Cushman, the Italian Ruffini, and the Greek Mousabines.
That is a mixed recollection from 1846 ; and it must have
been considerably after that date, as I calculate, but while
some of those named may have been still among the
*contubernales*, that De Quincey was first drawn into the
friendly circle.  The following anecdote of one of his appearances there is, therefore, only at secondhand :—To
suit some of the gentlemen, there had been produced on
this occasion, by special grace of the English hostess,
materials for the savage Scottish observance called whisky-
toddy.  In those days the orthodox instrument for mixing
the ingredients in the tumbler and conveying them thence
to the glass was a " toddy-ladle," generally of silver, but
preferably of wood.  Mrs. Crowe having apologized for the
absence of those articles and the substitution of mere tea-
spoons, De Quincey's politeness was moved to hyperbole.
" O, don't mention it, Mrs. Crowe," he said ; " don't
mention it ; for, if there is one thing in this world that I
abominate more than any other, it is those execrable
toddy-ladles."  There must be De Quinceyana a thousand
times better than this from some of the little *noctes* in
Darnaway Street and elsewhere from 1849 onwards, if
one could get at them.  But almost all De Quincey's

fellow-guests at such little gatherings are gone, as well as himself.

Any rare appearances, such as have been noted, of De Quincey at the table of an Edinburgh friend between 1849 and 1859 connect themselves, of course, with the Edinburgh focus of his little ellipse,—i.e. with Lothian Street. The more formal calls of visitors from a distance, British or American, were still almost invariably at Lass-wade, and naturally became fewer and fewer after the marriages of two of his daughters and the absences of the third made his own occasions for being there less frequent. Miss Martineau visited him in 1852, while all his daughters were still with him. She went away charmed by the exceptionally sweet audibility of his voice as it reached her through her ear-trumpet, and she lived to write a posthumous estimate of him, which might have been written more worthily. Mr. Fields, his American publisher, visited him about the same time, and could not afterwards say enough of his gentleness and courtesy of manner and the delights of his conversation. Another American, who visited him in 1854, transmits an anecdote which is worth more than general eulogium. The talk at the table had begun to veer round somehow to the subject of Scotland and the Scotch, when De Quincey, as if waking from a reverie, observed to the visitors that, as the servant who waited was a Scotch girl, he would be particularly obliged if they would reserve anything severe they had to say about the Scottish religion for moments when she should be out of the room. By far the best account, however, of a visit to De Quincey at Lasswade in his later years is one by the Rev. Francis Jacox. The visit, which was in July 1852, extended over some days, and included walks with De Quincey, as well as conver-

sations with him in the cottage.   Impressed, as everybody
was, with De Quincey's wonderful courtesy, the " sensitive
considerateness " of his style of address to all about him,
Mr. Jacox was particularly struck by the absence in him
of that habit of monologue which is the usual fault of
men celebrated for conversational power.   He was as
willing to listen as to talk.   Naturally, however, most of
the talk was left to *him*.   There were times of torpor or
dreaminess when he seemed incapable of anything ; but a
cup of coffee, or some less visible stimulus, would rouse
him like magic.   Then his talk would range over all
possible topics, from the gayest and lightest to the highest.
Mr. Jacox took note of some of his judgments in literary
matters.   He talked most affectionately of Wilson, who
was then broken down in health.   In speaking of Sir
William Hamilton and his metaphysics his strain rose to
nearly its highest mood, but with a reserve on behalf of
the later thinker Ferrier, as perhaps the subtler, if not so
learned and comprehensive.   He had read Isaac Taylor's
works, but did not care much about them.   With Miss
Edgeworth's novels he had much fault to find ; Dickens
he praised only *cum grano*, but preferred unhesitatingly
to Thackeray, on account of his more genial humanity ;
and against Thackeray's merits, Mr. Jacox thought, he
was mulishly obdurate.   He would not admire Emerson and
Hawthorne to the proper pitch, but had not then read the
best of Hawthorne.   He showed very considerable curiosity
about Maurice and Kingsley, and Christian Socialism, and
inquired very particularly about Mr. G. H. Lewes and his
London doings and employments.   He said that music
was a necessity of his daily life, and that, if he ever
visited London again, the opera would be his principal
attraction.   For the theatres in general he had little good

to say, and declared that he could hardly conceive of a
performance of a Shakespearian tragedy that should be
other than a profanation in his eyes ; but he spoke with
cordial admiration of Miss Helen Faucit as he had seen
her recently in Edinburgh in the part of Antigone. When
such conversations with De Quincey were out-of-doors,
in the country-roads about Lasswade, Mr. Jacox observed
that they were always beset or followed by beggars, and
that De Quincey gave something at once to every applicant, and always deferentially and with apology. The
last walk Mr. Jacox had with him was in seeing him so
far on his way back, on an evening, from Edinburgh to
Lasswade. While they were in Princes Street, De
Quincey showed a nervous anxiety lest any gesture of
himself or his companion should be construed by a cab-
man as an offer of a fare, and so bring him off the rank.
Some horrible experience seemed to be in his mind, and
he expressed his dread of " the overbearing brutality of
those men." The walk, so far as it was a joint concern,
ended at a point in the Meadows, where De Quincey
insisted that Mr. Jacox should turn back. Mr. Jacox
then bade him farewell, but watched his receding figure
as it disappeared up the lane, called Lovers' Loan, leading
from the Meadows to the rest of his long route over height
and hollow to Lasswade. He had opened a book of
Hawthorne's, which Mr. Jacox had given him, and was
reading it.

What more is to be known about De Quincey in his
last years is to be derived chiefly from those letters to his
daughters which, as has been mentioned, became touchingly frequent after the family had been dispersed. Mr.
Page has been able to publish a number of specimens,
and they have a very lively interest. It cannot be said,

indeed, that they admit us much to that "inner heart" of De Quincey the real nature of which so puzzled those who knew him best. With all his startling outside eccentricities, and even the glaring candours of his opium confessions, he remained an impenetrable being. Wilson himself could never explain him. What dark little core of a soul did his eccentricities conceal; or was there no real core of moral personality at all, but only a strange bunch or conformation of sensitive and intellectual nerves, over which the phenomena of the world could creep with the certainty of a keen response, and that could secrete thoughts and phantasies? The second supposition is irreconcilable with known facts. We have had signs already, and the writings furnish more in abundance, that the gentle, timid, shrinking, abnormally sensitive and polite little man was no more without his hard little bit of central self than other people, and that this might be found out on occasion. He had a very considerable fund of prejudice, temper, opinionativeness, animosity, pugnacity, on which he could draw when he liked; and sharp enough claws could be put forth from underneath the velvet. He had also, we need not doubt, his deeper hours and reveries of self-communing when De Quincey was alone with De Quincey, and more came out and was discoursed between them than friend or enemy could ever know. This mystery of the real De Quincey, however, has to be prosecuted through the whole biography and by means of the sum-total of the materials, and receives little elucidation from the private letters.

But, though these letters tell us little about De Quincey intrinsically that we should not have known otherwise, they let us see some traits of his character in the light of a peculiarly pleasant familiarity. Their fatherly and

K

grandfatherly fondness is really beautiful. We see the old man, late at night, in Lothian Street, amid his books and papers, stopping his work and pushing it aside, that he may shut his eyes and think for a while of his three girls, and of the little Eva and Johnny in the Irish home of one of them. The arrival of the post with letters from his daughters is the event of the twenty-four hours within which it occurs, and he likes nothing better than to prattle back to them by the next post. Here, how-ever, his difficulties, excuses, and explanations, are often comically absurd. Now he fears he has mislaid the letters just received; now he has but a single sheet of note-paper left, or has to write on a sheet of wretchedly coarse note-paper from a packet he had fortunately bought at the last shop he could find open on a Saturday night; now,—let his daughters exult with him!—he has "sprung a mine of envelopes" underneath the litter on his table, and will be at ease on that score for some time. Worst of all, it is quite uncertain whether the letter he is writing will ever be despatched ; for he knows he has written one already, which he cannot now find, and this one may disappear in like fashion, unless fate is propi-tious. When a letter did emerge from such throttling chances in its origin, it was pretty sure to be worth re-ceiving. With affectionate messages to the recipient and those about her, there might be chat about the progress of the Collected Edition of the Works, or about some in-cident in De Quincey's last walk or in the Lothian Street *ménage;* but in most cases the letter turned itself into a playful little dissertation, *à la De Quincey*, on some point of etymology or literature casually suggested. Once there was a minute account of a dream in which himself and two of his daughters were the figures, with an illustrative diagram to assist them in conceiving it exactly. That De Quincey took no ordinary interest in the current public news of the day we know independently; but the letters furnish additional proofs. We hear in them of second editions of the newspapers sent out for when anything of special moment was going on; and the amount of attention to the trial of Palmer in 1856 and to another famous case in 1857 answers to what we should expect from the author of the essay on " Murder considered as one of the Fine Arts." Nothing, however, seems to have interested De Quincey so much, or roused him so nearly to a paroxysm of personal excitement, as the Indian Mutiny of 1857-8. The fact that his daughter, Mrs. Baird Smith, and his son Paul Frederick, were then in India, and subsequently his pride in the share which fell to his son-in-law, Colonel Baird Smith, in the exertions for the suppression of the Mutiny, brought the tremendous story home to him, and made the impression of it the last great experience of his life.

Through the years of labour over the edition of the Collected Works De Quincey had been amusing himself with fresh literary projects. Mr. Hogg, after noting it as one of the peculiarities of his conversation that sometimes he would propound the most absurd things, and maintain them so gravely that it was impossible to say whether he was merely quizzing you and himself or might not be really in earnest, applies the remark especially to his persistence in bringing forward certain schemes of publishing adventure. While some of these alarmed Mr. Hogg by threatening interruption to the main labour, there was one which would not have been so chimerical in itself had time been left for it. This was a project of a new History of England in twelve volumes. After he was seventy he still harped on the project to Mr. Hogg, and longed for the conclusion of the Collective Edition, that he might begin the new work. He could finish it, he thought, in four years.

The autumn of 1859 had come, and the thirteenth volume of the Collected Works had been issued, and the fourteenth and last volume was all but ready for the press, when it became evident that De Quincey's work in the world was over. His life had gone to the extreme extent for which it had been wound up, and it was no definite malady, but the mere weakness of old age, that made him take to his bed. His youngest daughter, summoned from Ireland, where she had been on a visit to her sister, found him too feeble to bear removal to Lasswade, and remained with him in Lothian Street. Dr. Warburton Begbie, an Edinburgh physician of the highest celebrity at that day, was called in on the 22nd of October. He visited his patient latterly twice-a-day, finding him sometimes rallying so much as to be able to sit up or recline on a sofa, eager about what was in the day's newspapers, and trying to read them himself, or turning over the leaves of a new book. The perfect tranquillity of the patient, his anxiety not to give trouble, and the clearness with which he discussed the medical treatment of his case and the action of the remedies employed, especially with reference to the effects that might have been left on his constitution by opium, impressed Dr. Begbie greatly. There were, however, times of swooning and sleepy delirium, from which he seemed to awake with surprise. On such occasions his dreams seemed always to be of children. On Sunday the 4th of December the approach of death was so manifest that it was thought right to telegraph for Mrs. Craig, the only

other of his children then within reach. She arrived
in time to be recognised and welcomed; and on the
morning of Thursday, the 8th of December, the two
daughters standing by the bedside, and the physician
with them, De Quincey passed away. He had been in
a doze for some hours; and, as it had been observed
that in his waking hours since the beginning of his
illness he had reverted much to the incidents of his
childhood and talked especially of his father, regretting
that he had known so little of him, so in this final
doze his mind seemed to be wandering among the same
old memories. "My dear, dear mother : then I was
greatly mistaken," he was heard to murmur; and his
very last act was to throw up his arms and utter, as if
with a cry of surprised recognition, " Sister! Sister!
Sister!" The vision seemed to be that of his sister
Elizabeth, dead near Manchester seventy years before, and
now waiting for him on the banks of the river.

De Quincey, at the time of his death, was seventy-four
years and four months old. There were obituary notices
in the newspapers, but not nearly so numerous or loud
and elaborate as those which came out on the death of
Macaulay, at the age of fifty-nine, twenty days later in
the same month. Nor can I find that there was any great
attendance at De Quincey's funeral. He was buried in
the West Churchyard of Edinburgh, beside his wife and
two of their children; and on a tablet on a rather ruinous
part of one of the walls of that churchyard, at the end of
the bustling Princes Street and close under the Castle
Rock, one may read now this epitaph:—*Sacred to the
Memory of Thomas De Quincey, who was born at Greenhay, near Manchester, August 15th, 1785, and died in
Edinburgh, December 8th, 1859, and of Margaret, his wife,*

*who died August 7th*, 1837. The epitaph, it will be observed, preserves the blunder of most of the biographers as to the place of De Quincey's birth. What does it matter, or the poorness altogether of the monument ? Scott, whose monument is the central object of the city, and the finest ever reared anywhere in the world to a man of letters, was a native of Edinburgh ; Wilson, the noble bronze statue of whom attracts the eye in Princes Street, a little to the west of the Scott monument, was an Edinburgh citizen by adoption ; De Quincey, through three-fourths of his literary life belonging by accident to Edinburgh, was in no sense an Edinburgh man, and could expect no corresponding posthumous honours. Not one in two thousand of the inhabitants of Edinburgh at this moment knows where he is buried, or that he is buried in Edinburgh at all ; and not once in a year does any one of the select hundred who may be aware of the fact and the place think of visiting the humble grave. Again what does it matter? De Quincey's real constituency consists of all those, anywhere over the English-speaking world, who care for De Quincey's writings.

# CHAPTER XI.

ONE obvious distinction of De Quincey from most of the other chiefs of English Literature is that the writings by which he holds his high rank consist almost entirely of papers contributed to periodicals. Various books which he projected remained projects only ; and, with the exception of his *Logic of Political Economy*, now included among his collected works, and his novel called *Kloster-heim*, of which there has been no English reprint, all the products of his pen during the forty years of his literary life appeared originally in the pages of magazines or other serials. Just as Shakespeare may be described, in an off-hand manner, as the author of about thirty-seven plays, so may De Quincey be said to have taken his place in our Literature as the author of about 150 magazine articles.

Another obvious characteristic of De Quincey's writings is their extreme multifariousness. They range over an extraordinary extent of ground, the subjects of which they principally treat being themselves of the most diverse kinds, while their illustrative references and allusions shoot through a perfect wilderness of mis-cellaneous scholarship. This multifariousness of his matter is, in fact, but a manifestation of that peculiar personal character which chanced in his case to be brought into the business of literature. " For my own part, with

" out breach of truth or modesty," he says in one place,
" I may affirm that my life has been, on the whole, the
" life of a philosopher : from my birth, I was made an
" intellectual creature ; and intellectual in the highest
" sense my pursuits and pleasures have been, even from my
" schoolboy days." Again, in another place, he says :—" I
" have passed more of my life in absolute and unmitigated
" solitude, voluntarily, and for intellectual purposes, than
" any person of my age whom I have ever either met with,
" heard of, or read of." A stress, not intended by De
Quincey himself, may be laid on the word *intellectual* in
these passages. To hardly any one so little as to him
could there have been applied in his youth that observation which Goethe applied with such remarkable prescience
to Carlyle in the year 1827, when he defined him as " a
*moral* force of great importance," and added that, precisely
on account of this depth of the *moral* in his constitution,
it was impossible to foresee all that he would produce and
effect. No one could have said of De Quincey, at any
time of his life, that his strength lay in any predominance
of the moral element in his nature. On the contrary,
though severe enough in some of his criticisms on conduct,
and owning a distinct æsthetic preference for whatever is
lovely and of good report, he was defective in original
moral impetus or vehemence to a degree beyond the average.
It is no mere figure from grammar to say that few men
have come into the world, or have gone through it, with a
more meagre outfit of the imperative mood. It was because
he was so weak in this mood that we may call him so
specifically, in his own language, " an *intellectual* creature."
His main interest in life was that of universal curiosity,
sheer inquisitiveness and meditativeness about all things
whatsoever. Hence his early passion for the acquisition

of book-knowledge, and the fact that before his twenty-fifth year he had read so much and so variously as to be even then more entitled to the name of *polyhistor* than almost any of his English contemporaries.   Add that other store of knowledge which he had acquired by the exercise of a most subtle and insinuating faculty of observation upon human life and character around him, the "*quicquid agunt homines*" in all its varieties of "*votum, timor, ira, voluptas, gaudia, discursus*"; and add moreover a preternaturally tenacious memory; and it will be seen with what an unusual stock of materials De Quincey came to the craft of magazine authorship.   When he did so in his thirty-fifth year, it was under the compulsion of circumstances. He would rather not have adopted the craft; he would rather have gone on still as a private student and observer, with the chance of some outcome in laboured book-form at his own leisure; but, once harnessed to the periodical printing-press, he was at no loss for matter.   His command of German greatly increased in those days his range into the unhackneyed and uncommon; but, without that help, his extensive readings in the classics, in mediæval Latin, and in our earlier and less-known English authors, would have sufficed, in the grasp of a memory so retentive as his, to impart to his writings much of that polyhistoric character, that multifariousness of out-of-the-way learning, which we discern in them.

It is an important advance to be able to add that De Quincey's writings, so miscellaneous in their collective range, are all, or almost all, of high quality.   There are differences among them in this respect; but there is hardly one that does not, in the stereotyped phrase of reviewers, "well repay perusal."   Remembering this high general level of goodness through such a numerous series of articles,

and remembering the super-excellent goodness of not a
few, admirers of De Quincey are in the habit of saying
among themselves plaintively " Ah ! there is no such
writing nowadays ! " and have actually put the exclamation into print.  This is, in part, only the natural
exaggeration of loyalty to an old favourite ; and it forgets,
in the first place, what a quantity of very bad magazine-
writing there was in the days when De Quincey was at
his most brilliant in that business, and also what a quantity
of excellent writing there is in our magazines and reviews
at present.   But, in a rough way, the complaint seems to
hit a truth.   With some exceptions, there does seem to
be less of real mental exertion, less of notion that real
mental exertion is called for, in the magazine-writing and
review-writing of the present time than there was in the
palmy old days when De Quincey, Carlyle, Macaulay, and
some others, were doing their best in our monthlies and
quarterlies, and making their living by that species of
labour.   Anything does,—any kind of useful, or, as they
are beginning to call it, " informatory," printed matter, or
any compost of rough proximate ideas on a subject, or any
string of platitudes, repeating what nobody ever did not
know, if tinselled sufficiently into pretty sentences.   Not
unfrequently, when you have read the article of greatest
celebrity in the current number of a periodical, you find
that there has been no other motive to it than a theftuous
hope to amuse an hour for you after dinner by serving up to
you again the plums from some book which you and every
one else have read three weeks or a month before, the
entire drift of the article otherwise, and the whole substance
of its connecting paragraphs, not betraying the possession,
or at least the expenditure, of one quarter of an ounce of
real or original brain.   It is experience such as this that

makes one, so hastily, a *laudator temporis acti* in periodical
literature as in other matters, and drives one back to De
Quincey's sixteen volumes or to any similar collection,
with such angry forgetfulness of the fact that these collections themselves are but the solid monuments remaining
from amid acres of vanished rubbish. The forgetfulness
is wrong, but the result for readers may happen to be
beneficial. De Quincey's sixteen volumes of magazine articles
are full of brain from beginning to end. At the rate of
about half a volume a day, they would serve for a month's
reading, and a month continuously might be worse expended.
There are few courses of reading from which a young man of
good natural intelligence would come away more instructed,
charmed, and stimulated, or, to express the matter as
definitely as possible, with his mind more *stretched*.
Good natural intelligence, a certain fineness of fibre, and
some amount of scholarly education, have to be pre-
supposed, indeed, in all readers of De Quincey. But, even
for the fittest readers, a month's complete and continuous
course of De Quincey would be too much. Better have him
on the shelf, and take down a volume at intervals for one or
two of the articles to which there may be an immediate
attraction. An evening with De Quincey in this manner
will always be profitable.

Not only was it De Quincey's laudable habit to put
brain into all his articles, but it so chanced that the brain
he had at his disposal was a brain of no common order.
Let us get rid, however, of the disagreeable word *brain*,
and ask, in more manly and less physiological fashion, what
were the chief characteristics of De Quincey's peculiar mind
and genius. At the basis of all, as we have seen, was his
learning, his wealth of miscellaneous and accurate knowledge. On that topic enough has been said ; and we advert

to it again only because it is well to remember that, whatever else De Quincey was, he was at all events a scholar and polyhistor.

But what was he besides ?   He was distinguished from most modern specimens of the genus *polyhistor* by the possession, in the first place, of a singularly independent, clear, subtle, exact, and penetrating intellect. The independence of his intellect is in itself remarkable.  No one was less disposed to take common opinions on trust, no one more keenly sceptical in his general judgments, no one more ready to challenge a popular or even a scholastic tradition on any subject, reinvestigate the evidence, and persist in getting at the root of the matter for himself.   His strength in this quality has been called love of paradox, and sometimes it does go to that length.  As he himself explained, however, a paradox is properly not something incredible, but only something beyond the bounds of present belief; and it is remarkable how often, when he is followed in one of his so-called paradoxes, he turns out to be right.   Sometimes, when this happens, one finds that it was the mere exercise of shrewd common sense, a rapid deductive perception from the first of what *must* be the case in the circumstances, that enabled him to challenge the common opinion ; but more frequently it is his historical knowledge that serves him, his power of marshalling facts inductively and interpreting their relations.   But, even when he fails to convince, he always instructs, always suggests something that remains in the mind and goes on working, never leaves a question exactly as it was.   One is reminded in reading him of Goldsmith's saying about Burke's conversation in contrast with Johnson's.   Admiring Johnson's extraordinary powers in that way as much as any man, but irritated by Boswell's perpetual harping on the theme,

" Is he like Burke, sir, who winds into a subject like a
serpent ? " Goldsmith was once moved to ask.    Now,
this serpentine insinuation of himself into the heart of a
subject, rather than Johnson's direct and broadside style
of attack upon a subject externally, was De Quincey's
usual method.  He generally knows his conclusion from the
first, and sometimes announces it dogmatically at the out-
set ; but, whether for inquiry towards his conclusion or for
proof of it after it has been announced, his habit is to
choose a point of entry, and thence, by subtle and intricate
windings, to reach the centre, where the concurrent trains
will meet, and all will become clear.    His windings have
often the appearance of wilful digressions, and digressive-
ness is the fault with which he is most commonly charged.
It was perhaps the same labyrinthine habit, or at all events
the tendency to long-spun threads of reasoning, that
Carlyle had in view when he applied the epithet " wire-
drawn " to some of De Quincey's mental products.    His
digressions, however, to use his own phrase, have a wonderful
knack of *revolving* to the point whence they set out, and
generally with a fresh freight of meaning to be incorporated
at that point ; and, so far as one might acquiesce in the
description of some of De Quincey's mental products as
" wire-drawn," it is in cases where one might agree with
Carlyle that the kind of matter dealt with was not worth
so much manipulation, and that simple assumption or
asseveration, or decision by a toss-up, would have saved
time and answered all practical purposes.    Very rarely,
however, will one of De Quincey's subtlest ingenuities
be voted useless by any reader who does come qualified
with the due amount of preliminary interest in the kind
of matter discussed,—so much pleasure is there in observing the ingenuity itself, and so certain is it, as has been

already said, that some germ of future thought will be
left if the immediate result has been disappointing.   Then
with what a passion for scientific exactness does De
Quincey treat everything, and in what a state of finished
clearness at the end he leaves every speculation of his,
so far as it may have been carried !  His numerical
divisions and subdivisions, so unusual in literary papers,
are themselves signs of the practised thinker, refusing to
part with any of the habits or devices of scientific analysis
wherever they will help him.   In short, very seldom has
there been such a combination of the purely logical
intellect with so much of scholarly erudition.

De Quincey's intellect, while keenly analytic and exact,
was also very rich and inventive.   The distinction will
be understood by remembering the essays and disquisitions
of Bacon, Sir Thomas Browne, Jeremy Taylor, Burke, or
Coleridge, in contrast with those of such thinkers as
Locke, Bishop Butler, David Hume, James Mill, or Sir
William Hamilton.  That the distinction does not coincide
with that into the two opposed philosophical schools will
have appeared from the mixture of names.   Neither does
it connect itself with any distinction of emotional temperaments among thinkers, as into the cool and the fervid.
There may be a fervid thinker whose manner of thinking
is of the plain and straightforward sort ; and there may
be a cool thinker whose manner of thinking, while equally
scientific and precise, is at the same time rich and inventive.    Nor does Bacon's distinction between *lumen siccum*
or dry light, and *lumen humidum*, or light drenched in
the affections and customs, correspond exactly with what
is meant ; nor does the ordinary distinction between the
non-poetic and the poetic, though that comes nearer.  The
distinction is purely one of intellectual manner, and may

be seen where there is identity in the substance of the thought to be expressed. Some writers, knowing what they mean to say beforehand, say it nakedly and rigidly, with nothing additional or subsidiary; others, meaning the same thing, and equally knowing what they mean beforehand, cannot put it forth without putting forth also a good deal more that has been generated in the very act of thinking it out, and that, while organically related to it, may be independently interesting. De Quincey belongs, in the main, to the latter class. As he had a teeming memory, so he had, as he tells us himself, "an electric aptitude for seizing analogies," or, as he again expresses it more fully, "a logical instinct for feeling in a moment the secret analogies or parallelisms that connect things else apparently remote." Hence that quality of his thought which we have called richness or inventiveness. In the act of thinking anything, metonymies, metaphors, anecdotes, illustrations historical or fantastic, start up in his mind, become incorporate with his primary thought, and are, in fact, its language. It will not do to call this, as some have proposed, the literary mode of treating a subject, and to call the bleaker mode the strictly scientific; for the former may be as strictly scientific, as valid and effective logically, as the latter. It would not be difficult, at all events, were a specimen passage of exposition or reasoning produced from a modern English writer of the more arid and rigid order, to produce from De Quincey, if the same topic should be really within his province and he should chance to have treated it, a parallel passage in *his* richer style beating his rigid brother's out of sight for logical precision and clearness, perfection of impression on the pure understanding. Nevertheless, as it is the richer and more inventive style of writing that succeeds best in

producing what, while serving the purposes of philosophical or scientific exposition, will take rank also distinctively as a piece of *literature*, there is no harm in saying
that De Quincey's intellect was in the main of the literary
order.   In most of his papers it is professedly as a man of
letters, remembering the aims and objects of literature
proper, and seeking to touch the general human heart, that
he handles philosophical or other speculative problems.
Hence those egotisms, those frequent Montaigne-like confidences between himself and his readers as he proceeds,
which, as part of his passion for introducing whatever of
general human interest can be made relative to a subject
or can brighten and illustrate it, give to his most abstract
dissertations such a character of individuality or De
Quinceyism.   There are cases, his greatest admirers must
admit, in which the subsidiary swallows up the primary,
and the captain's luggage all but sinks the ship and cargo.
For example, it is rather provoking to a short temper, in a
paper on Sir William Hamilton and his Philosophy, to
find the exordium consisting of a long complaint about the
postal difficulties between Lasswade and Edinburgh, and
the same subject and others equally irrelevant recurring
*ad libitum* throughout, while poor Sir William is kept
waiting in a corner and is fetched out of it only at
intervals. The only excuse in such cases is that De Quincey
seems to have understood it to be bargained between himself and his readers that, whatever title he gave to a paper,
he was to be the sole judge of what it should turn out to
be, provided the sum-total should be sufficiently amusing.
Very rarely, however, is any such excuse needed.   While
it does seem to have been a canon with De Quincey, in
the preparation of his articles, that the sum-total of each
should be interesting by some means or other, and while

very often an article is not quite what would have been expected from the title, it is astonishing how habitually, in the hurry of magazine-writing, he contrived to redeem and justify his title, keep his real subject in hand through all seeming involutions and digressions, return with artistic fidelity to the key-note, and leave all at the end, as we have said, in a state of finished clearness.

There was in De Quincey's genius, as all know, a very considerable vein of humour. A sense of fun follows him into his most serious disquisitions, and reveals itself in freaks of playfulness and jets of comic fancy; and once or twice, as in his *Murder considered as one of the Fine Arts,* he breaks into sheer extravagance or wild and pro-tracted rollick. Even then it cannot be said that his humour is of the largest-hearted kind, so dependent is it on deliberate irony, a Petronian jostling of the ghastly with the familiar, or the express simulation of lunacy. In its display on the smaller scale, as diffused through his writings, it is generally good-natured and kindly. It is not to be denied, however, that there was an ingredient of the mischievous or Mephistophelic in De Quincey's tem-per, which could show itself occasionally under the guise of his usually gentle humour. He could never have been " a good hater," his equipment of moral energy being too languid for that; but there are parts and passages of his writings that leave the impression of a something which it would be difficult to distinguish from spite and malevolence.

Humour and pathos, we have been told, are twins and inseparable. However that may be, De Quincey's en-dowment in pathos was certainly not less than his endowment in humour. From his earliest infancy, as we saw, a sense of the manifold miseries of life had been

L

impressed upon him by his own experience and observation, and had settled in him into a kind of brooding
melancholy. Not only such common calamities as
bereavement, disease, physical pain, poverty, oppression,
misconstruction, contempt, but the rarer and more secret
forms of anguish that belong to peculiar temperaments
and fatal shocks of circumstance, had been meditated by
him, with the diligence of a constitutional bias to that
sombre field of study, and with continued aids from his
own troubles, till he had become a master in the whole
science of sorrow. In particular, that early discovery which
had first made the word *Pariah* so significant to him, the
discovery of the omnipresence of inherited and unre-
garded misery, in specks or in masses, on the skirts of
smiling society, or actually within its bosom, had accompanied him all his life long, till the word *Pariah* had
become, as we noted, one of the most indispensable
words in his vocabulary, and the corresponding notion one
of his forms of thought. In his personal behaviour,
feeble as it was practically, this recollection of the
miserable and dismal on all sides of him, this incessant
wandering of his thoughts to the slave, the pauper, the
lazar, the criminal, the street-outcast, and the maniac,
had shown itself in a kind of constant anti-Pharisaism,
a constant self-humiliation and pity for the abject.
Why should he abhor, why should he condemn, why
should he stand aloof, why should he refuse alms, or
institute very rigid inquiries before giving : what was he
himself that he should be punctilious ? This mood, and
the theme which occasioned it, he carried into his writings.
There too one finds a habitual recollection of the variety
and immensity of suffering diffused through life ; and
there too the inclination of the teaching, in the matter of

the ways and means of dealing with crime and misery, is always towards what is commonly called "the sentimental," but some would call "the Christian." Hence also, in part, the frequent tendency to the lyrical and plaintive in the cast of De Quincey's language.

There was yet a grander source of this tendency to the lyrical in his feeling for the mysterious and sublime. It was a saying of his own that he could not live without mystery. No man that is worth much can. If all humanity could be rolled into one soul, to think and feel as such, then, all those activities and necessities having been abolished which arise from the very fact that it is distributed or disparate, into what mood could it settle and be absorbed but that of wondering speculation into its own origin? On this very account, is not this mood, which may be called the metaphysical mood, the most essentially and specifically *human* of all moods? Most people have no time for it; they have too much to do; but he is hardly a man who does not fall into it sometimes; and it is nursed in some into abnormal intensity by constitutional aptitude and by habits of solitude. De Quincey was one of these. He was wrapt in a general religious wonder; he went through the world, one may say, in a fit of metaphysical musing. But not only was he occupied, as all such minds are, with the great objects of religious contemplation in its most abstract reaches towards the invisible, and with the standing metaphysical problems connected with those objects; his sense of mystery fastened also on all those elementary sublimities in nature or life which, by their pre-eminent power over the human imagination, seem like the chief irruptions of the invisible and supernatural into the sphere of man. The thunder and the lightning, the sun in the heavens, the nocturnal sky, the quiet vastness of a mountain-range, the roar of the unresting ocean, the carnage of a great battle-field, the stealthy ravage of a pestilence, the tramp of a multitude in insurrection, a Joan of Arc heroic and death-defying before her judges, Cæsar at the Rubicon when the world hung on his decision and there came upon him the phrenzy to cross,—such were the physical grandeurs, and such the facts and moments of historic majesty, with which De Quincey's mind delighted to commune, as if seeing in them the clearest messages from infinitude and the most startling intimations of the intermingling of the demoniacal with the divine.· Yet another descent, however, and we find his passion for mystery taking relief even in the wizardly and necromantic. Among the passages of his early reading which had struck him with an effect so extraordinary that he could account for it only by supposing that they had wakened special affinities in his constitution, he mentions particularly the opening scene in *Macbeth* :—

> *A Desert Place. Thunder and Lightning. Enter three Witches.*
>
> *First Witch.*　When shall we three meet again,
> 　　　　　　　In thunder, lightning, or in rain?
> *Second Witch.*　When the hurly-burly's done,
> 　　　　　　　When the battle's lost and won.
> *Third Witch.*　That will be ere the set of sun.

It would be difficult for any one not to carry away something of the feeling of this passage, and hundreds of thousands have done so; but what we observe in De Quincey is that he carried away the feeling and retained it in that form of a permanent tenet which it seems to have held in Shakespeare's own creed : viz., in the form of a postulate for the imagination, if not for the reason, of

the interference in human affairs of other and more occult
agencies than are dreamt of in the ordinary philosophy.
No one, indeed, could be more humorously pungent on
all superstitions of the witchcraft order than De Quincey
was.  He took special pleasure in showing how, by the
application of mathematics and physical tests, the most
pretentious of those superstitions, such as Astrology, could
be blasted into nonsense.  But this does not prevent our
detecting in him a lurking fondness for some personal
variety of the doctrine of a possible interfusion of the non-
human or quondam-human with the known life of the
present.  Perhaps the best name for this variety of the affection for the mysterious in De Quincey's mind is Druidism
or the Druidic element.  It is a more common element in
British genius, and perhaps a more respectable, than is
generally supposed.  It reveals itself in De Quincey in
his fondness for noting dreams, omens, casual symbolisms,
marvellous coincidences, anticipations or prophecies of
death, and the like, and also in his liking for such subjects
of historical investigation as secret societies, Freemasonry,
Rosicrucianism, and the Pagan Oracles.

To be noted, finally, in this enumeration of De Quincey's
characteristics, is the prominence in his genius of the
special faculty of poetic imagination.  Though involved
partly in what has just been said as to the strength of his
feeling for the mysterious and sublime, and also in what
was formerly said as to the richness and inventiveness of
his manner of thinking on any subject, this remark is
really independent.  The feeling for the mysterious and
sublime is a natural cause of poetic conception, and a
habit of poetic conception will contribute, with other
things, to richness or literary charm in the treatment of a
subject ; but the poetic faculty, in its distinct and special

form, is the faculty of continuous constructive dreaming, of "bodying forth the forms of things unknown," of turning meanings and feelings into actual "shapes," i. e. into visual and representative phantasies. In what large measure De Quincey possessed this faculty, and how conscious he was that the specimens of it he had left might be one of his distinctions among English prose-writers, are as generally known as the fact of his opium-eating, and are indeed often connected with that fact in recollections of him.

In an essay on "The Genius of De Quincey" Mr. Shad-worth Hodgson, who knew him personally, vouches that no description of him could surpass for exactness that provided beforehand by the poet Thomson in the stanza of his *Castle of Indolence* in which he introduces the bard Philomelus :—

> He came, the bard, a little Druid wight
> Of withered aspect ; but his eye was keen,
> With sweetness mixed.   In russet brown bedight,
> As is his sister of the copses green,
> He crept along, unpromising of mien.
> Gross he who judges so !   His soul was fair,
> Bright as the children of yon azure sheen.
> True comeliness, which nothing can impair,
> Dwells in the mind : all else is vanity and glare.

The quotation is a happy one, and entitles Mr. Hodgson to our thanks.   By this time, however, we ought to know our little Druid wight somewhat more intimately than by his external appearance.   It remains only to say something about his English style.

In no case is there better proof or illustration than in De Quincey's of the important principle of the radical identity of style and thought, the impossibility of separating them in ultimate theory, and the mischief of the common habit of conceiving otherwise.  In writing or speaking, it is not as if you first obtained your thought, and then looked about for a mantle in which to dress it, and might choose the mantle coarse or fine, loose or tight, green or purple.  The mantle itself, every fibre of it, is a fabrication of thinkings and feelings, coming into existence by the very action and motion of that main thought or feeling which you call the core or substance, and organically united with it, and partaking of all its qualities.  To change your style is to change your mode of thinking; nay, to change the kind of matter that you will allow to come into your mind.  All those characteristics of De Quincey's mind that have been enumerated reproduce themselves, therefore, as characteristics of his style, and may be observed and studied afresh under that name.  Hence too an excellency in him that ought to be found in every writer who ranges over any considerable variety of subjects,—to wit, a versatility of style, a change in the character of the wording and the syntax, from the simple and plain to the richer and more involved, answering to every change in the matter, mood, or purpose.  To write always in an easy conversational style means never to allow anything to come into the mind that could not be generated in the course of easy conversation with a friend or two,—which, as friends now go, would be hard news for philosophy, poetry, and a few other things that are considered not unimportant ; to try to write always like Goldsmith or Charles Lamb means to beg to have your mind taken back and remelted into the precise mould of Goldsmith's or Charles Lamb's,—which might be an exchange in your favour, but is impossible ; to write always in good old Saxon English and eschew Latin and Greek words means to abstain from traffic with all objects and notions that have come into the cognisance of the English intellect since the time of King Harold, or else to make yourself a scarecrow and laughing-stock, and forswear some of the noblest glories of your composite nationality, by rigging yourself up in imagined equivalents from the vocabulary of Cedric and Gurth the swineherd. All the same, while there ought to be this expectation of variety in the style of a writer, according to his subject and purpose, it remains true that every writer has, on the whole, a style of his own. He is discernible from others by his style, just as, and just because, he is discernible from others by the total contour of that combination of mental qualities which is called his genius. Like most other traditional and time-honoured distinctions, the distinction between thought and style is practically valuable; it is indeed indispensable in criticism; but the reason is that the study of a writer's style is, in fact, one way, and the most obvious way, of becoming minutely acquainted with his mental resources and processes. Style is mental behaviour from moment to moment; and, if it involves such a thing as a self-imposed rule or rhythm, then that rule or rhythm is itself a function of the mind that imposes it, contents included as well as habits.

The style of De Quincey, as might be expected, is prevailingly intellectual. There is nothing tempestuous in it; we are not hurried along by any excess of rage or other animating passion. Even when his pathos or his feeling of the mysterious and sublime is at its highest, and the strain accordingly becomes most lyrical, we are aware of the presence of a keen intellectual perceptiveness, an artistic self-possession, a power of choosing and reasoning among different means towards a desired effect. It is a beautiful style, uniquely De Quincey's, the characteristic of which, in its more level and easy specimens, is intellectual nimbleness, a light precision and softness of spring, while in the higher specimens, where the movement becomes more involved and intricately rhythmical, there is still the same sense of a leisurely intellectual instinct, rather than glow and rapture, as regulating the feat. If one could fancy such a thing as a flow of ivy or other foliage, rich, soft, and glancing, but not too dense, advancing quietly over a surface and covering it equably, but with a power of shooting itself rapidly to selected points and pinnacles, *that* might be an image of De Quincey's language overspreading a subject. It moves quietly, enfolding all it meets with easy grace, and leaving a vesture pleasantly soft and fine, rather than gaudily-varied or obtrusive ; but it can collect itself into rings of overgrowth, or shoot into devices and festoons. Very often, when the subject is simple, when it is an ordinary piece of description or explanation that is on hand, the phrasing is familiar and colloquial, with short and simple sentences to correspond, though even then with a scholarly tact for neatness and accuracy, a quest of liveliness and elegance, and a wonderful power of alighting on the exact word that is fittest. The tendency of De Quincey, however, as all know, is to subjects of a recondite order, and to the recondite in all subjects ; and hence what is usually remembered as De Quincey's style is that style of more stately complexity, with long evolutions and harmonies of sentence, and free resort to all the wealth of the Latin element in our tongue, of which his more elaborate writings are examples. On this subject of the " elaborate " style a quotation from himself, reflecting on the style of Hazlitt and Charles Lamb, may be relevant :—

Hazlitt was not eloquent, because he was discontinuous. No

man can be eloquent whose thoughts are abrupt, insulated, capricious, and (to borrow an impressive word from Coleridge) non-sequacious. Eloquence resides not in separate or fractional ideas, but in the relations of manifold ideas, and in the mode of their evolution from each other. It is not indeed enough that the ideas should be many, and their relations coherent; the main condition lies in the *key* of the evolution, in the *law* of the succession. The elements are nothing without the atmosphere that moulds, and the dynamic forces that combine. Now, Hazlitt's brilliancy is seen chiefly in separate splinterings of phrase or image, which throw upon the eye a vitreous scintillation for a moment, but spread no deep suffusions of colour, and distribute no masses of mighty shadow. A flash, a solitary flash, and all is gone. . . . Hazlitt's thoughts were of the same fractured and discontinuous order as his illustrative images,— seldom or never self-diffusive; and *that* is a sufficient argument that he had never cultivated philosophic thinking. . . . We are bound to acknowledge that Lamb thought otherwise on this point, manifesting what seemed to us an extravagant admiration of Hazlitt, and perhaps even in part for that very glitter which we are denouncing; at least he did so in conversation with ourselves. But, on the other hand, as this conversation travelled a little into the tone of a disputation, and *our* frost on this point might seem to justify some undue fervour by way of balance, it is very possible that Lamb did not speak his absolute and dispassionate judgment. And yet again, if he *did*, may we, with all reverence for Lamb's exquisite genius, have permission to say that his own intellect sinned by this very habit of discontinuity? . . . He himself, we fear, not bribed by indulgent feelings to another, not moved by friendship, but by native tendency, shrank from the continuous, from the sustained, from the elaborate. The elaborate, indeed, without which much truth and beauty must perish in germ, was by name the object of his invectives. The instances are many, in his own beautiful essays, where he literally collapses, literally sinks away from openings suddenly offering themselves to flights of pathos or solemnity in direct prosecution of his own theme. On any such summons, where an ascending impulse

and an untired pinion were required, he *refuses* himself (to use
military language) invariably. The least observing reader of
*Elia* cannot have failed to notice that his most felicitous
passages always accomplish their circuit in a few sentences.
The gyration within which his sentiment wheels, no matter of
what kind it may be, is always the shortest possible. It does
not prolong itself, it does not repeat itself, it does not propagate
itself. . . . We ourselves, occupying the very station of polar
opposition to that of Lamb, being as morbidly, perhaps, in the
one excess as he in the other, naturally detected this omission
in Lamb's nature at an early stage of our acquaintance. Not
the famed Regulus, with his eyelids torn away, and his un-
curtained eyeballs exposed to the noontide glare of a Cartha-
ginian sun, could have shrieked with more anguish of recoil
from torture than we from certain sentences and periods in
which Lamb perceived no fault at all. *Pomp*, in our appre-
hension, was an idea of two categories; the *pompous* might be
spurious, but it might also be genuine. It is well to love the
simple,—*we* love it; nor is there any opposition at all between
*that* and the very glory of pomp. But, as we once put the case
to Lamb, if, as a musician, as the leader of a mighty orchestra,
you had this theme offered to you,—" Belshazzar the king gave
a great feast to a thousand of his lords,"—or this, "And on a
certain day Marcus Cicero stood up, and in a set speech rendered
thanks to Caius Cæsar for Quintus Ligarius pardoned and
Marcus Marcellus restored,"—surely no man would deny that
in such a case simplicity, though in a passive sense not lawfully
absent, must stand aside as totally insufficient for the *positive*
part.

A great deal of De Quincey's best and most characteristic
writing is in the stately and elaborate style here described,
the style of sustained splendour, of prolonged wheeling
and soaring, as distinct from the style of crackle and brief
glitter, of chirp and short flight. This is precisely on
account of the exalted and intricate nature of his meaning
and feeling in those cases; and, if some readers there fall
off from him or dislike him, it is because they themselves

are deficient in wing and sinew. For those who do adhere
to him and follow him in his passages of more involved
and sustained eloquence, there are few greater pleasures
possible in modern English prose. However magnificent
the wording, there is always such an exact fit between it
and the amount and shape of the under-fluctuating thought
that suspicion of inflation or bombast anywhere never
occurs to one. The same presence everywhere of a vigilant
intellect appears in the perfect logical articulation of
sentence with sentence and of clause with clause ; while
the taste of the technical artist appears equally in the
study of minute optical coherence in the imagery and in
the fastidious care for fine sound. In this last quality of
style,—to which, in its lowest degree, Bentham gave the
name of *pronunciability,* insisting most strenuously on
its ·importance in all writing,—De Quincey is a master.
Such was the delicacy of his ear, however, that mere
*pronunciability* was not enough for him, and *musical beauty*
had to be superadded. Once, writing of Father Newman,
and having described him as " originally the ablest son of
Puseyism, but now a powerful architect of religious
philosophy on his own account," he interrupts himself to
explain that he might have ended the sentence more
briefly by substituting for the last nine words the single
phrase " master-builder," but that his ear could not
endure " a sentence ending with two consecutive trochees,
and each of those trochees ending with the same syllable
*er.*" He adds, " Ah reader ! I would the gods had made
thee rhythmical, that thou mightest comprehend the
thousandth part of my labours in the evasion of cacophony." The last phrase, " the evasion of cacophony,"
is an instance of another of De Quincey's verbal habits in
his more elaborate writing,—his deliberate choice now and

then of an unusually learned combination of Latin or
Greek or other polysyllabic words.  Often, as in the present instance, it is a whim of mere humour or self-irony.
Often, however, it is from a desire to be exact to his
meaning and to leave that meaning indissolubly associated
with the word or phrase that does most closely express it.
Occasionally, as when he speaks of " the crepuscular ante-
lucan worship " of the Essenes, or of a sentence as being
liable to "a whole nosology of malconformations," or of
the importance attached to the mystery of baptism among
our forefathers as "shown by the multiplied *ricochets*
through which it impressed itself upon their vocabulary,"
it will depend on the temper and the intellectual alertness
of the reader at the moment whether the phrase is accepted
or voted needlessly quaint and abstruse ; but most of his
Latinisms or other neologisms do recommend themselves
as at once luminous and tasteful, and it is hardly to
them that exception is taken by his most severe critics.
They object rather to certain faults to which he is liable
in those portions of his writings where he affects the brisk
and popular.  By a kind of reaction from his other extreme
of stateliness, he is then apt to be too familiar and colloquial, and to help himself to slang and kitchen-rhetoric.
He will speak of a thing as "smashed,"—which is too
violent for the nerves of those who cannot bear to see a
thing "smashed," but prefer that it should be "broken in
pieces " or "reduced to fragments"; he will interject such
an exclamation as " O crimini ! ",—which is unpardonable
in sedate society ;  he will take the Jewish historian
Josephus by the button, address him as "Joe" through a
whole article, and give him a black eye into the bargain,
—which is positively profane.  In most such cases one
does not see why De Quincey should not have the same

liberty as Swift or Thackeray; but it must be admitted
that sometimes the joke is feeble and the slang unpleasant.  In excuse one has to remember that a magazine-
writer is often driven to shifts.  And, slips of taste in the
vocabulary discounted, how many magazine-writers will
compete with De Quincey in the accuracy, the disciplined
accuracy, of his grammar?  His pointing in itself is a
testimony to the logical clearness of his intellect; and I have
found no single recurring fault of syntax in his style, unless it be in his sanction of a very questionable use of the
English participle.  " No Christian state could be much
in advance of another, *supposing* that Popery opposed no
barriers to free communication," is an example of a frequent construction with De Quincey, which I wish he had
avoided.  As he has not, the benefit of his authority may
be claimed for that apparent slovenliness of an unrelated
or misrelated participle which, by some fiction of an elliptical
case-absolute, or of transmutation of the participial form
into a conjunction or adverb, passes as consistent with the
free genius of our uninflected language.  But it jars on a
classic sense of grammar, and is wholly unnecessary.[1]

[1] For a minute and instructive study of the mechanism of De
Quincey's style, I may refer to Professor Minto's *Manual of
English Prose Literature*.

# CHAPTER XII.

DE QUINCEY'S WRITINGS : CLASSIFICATION AND REVIEW.

How are De Quincey's writings to be classified ? His own classification, propounded in the General Preface to the edition of his Collected Works, was to the effect that they might be distributed roughly into three sorts,—*first*, those papers of fact and reminiscence the object of which was primarily to amuse the reader, though they might reach to a higher interest, e. g. the *Autobiographic Sketches ; secondly*, essays proper, or papers addressing themselves purely or primarily to " the understanding as an insulated faculty," e. g. *The Essenes*, *The Cæsars*, and *Cicero ;* and, *thirdly*, that " far higher class of compositions " which might be considered as examples of a very rare kind of " impassioned prose," e. g. large portions of *The Confessions of an Opium-Eater* and the supplementary *Suspiria de Profundis*. This classification, though not quite the same as Bacon's division of the " parts of learning " (by which he meant " kinds of literature ") into History or the Literature of Memory, Philosophy or the Literature of Reason, and Poetry or the Literature of Imagination, is practically equivalent. Hence, as Bacon's classification is the more scientific and searching, and also the most familiar and popular, we shall be pretty safe in adopting it, and dividing De Quincey's writings into :—(I.) Writings of Reminiscence, or Descriptive, Biographical, and Historical

Writings; (II.) Speculative, Didactic, and Critical Writings;
(III.) Imaginative Writings and Prose-Poetry. It is
necessary, above all things, to premise that in De Quincey
the three sorts of writing shade continually into each
other. Where this difficulty of the constant blending of
kinds in one and the same paper is not met by the obvious
preponderance of one of the kinds, it may be obviated by
naming some papers in more divisions than one. With
that understanding, we proceed to a classified synopsis of
De Quincey's literary remains :—

## I. DESCRIPTIVE, BIOGRAPHICAL, AND HISTORICAL.

The writings of this class may be enumerated and
subdivided as follows :—

I. AUTOBIOGRAPHIC :—Specially of this kind are *The Confessions of an English Opium-Eater* and the *Autobiographic
Sketches;* but autobiographic matter is dispersed through
other papers.

II. BIOGRAPHIC SKETCHES OF PERSONS KNOWN TO THE
AUTHOR :—Some such are included in the autobiographic
writings ; but distinct papers of the kind are *Recollections of
the Lake Poets, or Sketches of Coleridge, Wordsworth, and
Southey,* and the articles entitled *Coleridge and Opium-
Eating, Charles Lamb, Professor Wilson, Sir William
Hamilton, Walking Stewart, Note on Hazlitt,* and *Dr. Parr,
or Whiggism in its Relations to Literature.* All these papers
are partly critical. Several papers of the same sort that appeared in magazines have not been reprinted in the Collective
British Edition.

III. OTHER BIOGRAPHIC SKETCHES :—*Shakespeare* (in
Vol. XV.), *Milton* (in Vol. X.), *Pope* (in Vol. XV.), *Richard
Bentley, Percy Bysshe Shelley, The Marquis Wellesley, Last
Days of Immanuel Kant* (a digest from the German), *Lessing,
Herder, Goethe* (in Vol. XV.), *Schiller.* These also include
criticism with biography.

IV. HISTORICAL SKETCHES AND DESCRIPTIONS :—*Homer*

*and the Homeridæ, Philosophy of Herodotus, Toilette of the Hebrew Lady* (archæological), *The Cæsars* (in six chapters, forming the greater part of Vol. IX.), *Charlemagne, Revolt of the Tartars, The Revolution of Greece, Modern Greece, Ceylon, China* (a little essay on the Chinese character, with illustrations), *Modern Superstition, Anecdotage, French and English Manners, Account of the Williams Murders* (the *postscript* to "Murder considered as one of the Fine Arts"). In the same sub-class we would include the two important papers entitled *Rhetoric* and *Style;* for, though to a considerable extent critical and didactic, they are, despite their titles, chiefly surveys of Literary History.

V. HISTORICAL SPECULATIONS AND RESEARCHES :—In this class may be included *Cicero, The Casuistry of Roman Meals, Greece under the Romans, Judas Iscariot, The Essenes, The Pagan Oracles, Secret Societies, Historico-Critical Inquiry into the Origin of the Rosicrucians and Freemasons, Ælius Lamia.*

The two Autobiographic volumes and the volume of Reminiscences of Coleridge, Wordsworth, and Southey, are among the best-known of De Quincey's writings. Among the other biographic sketches of persons known to him *Charles Lamb, Walking Stewart,* and *Dr. Parr* are those of the highest merit,—the last very severe and satirical, but full of interest and of marked ability. Of the other biographic sketches the ablest and most interesting by far is *Richard Bentley,* a really splendid specimen of biography in miniature. The Encyclopædia article on *Shakespeare,* though somewhat thin, deserves notice for the perfection of its proportions as a summary of what is essential in our information respecting Shakespeare's life. It is not yet superannuated. The similar article on *Pope* is interesting as an expression of De Quincey's generous admiration all in all of a poet whom he treats very severely in detail in some of his critical papers ; and it is rare

M

to meet so neat and workmanlike a little curiosity as the paper on *The Marquis Wellesley*. Of the personal sketches of eminent Germans, that entitled *The Last Days of Immanuel Kant*, though it is only a translated digest from a German original, bears the palm for delicious richness of anecdote and vividness of portraiture. De Quincey's credit in it, except in so far as he shaped and changed and infused life while translating (which was a practice of his), rests on the fact that he was drawn to the subject by his powerful interest in Kant's philosophy, and conceived the happy idea of such a mode of creating among his countrymen a personal affection for the great abstract thinker. Some of the other German sketches, especially *Lessing* and *Herder*, have the same special merit of being early and useful attempts to introduce some knowledge of German thought and literature into England; but the *Goethe*, on all accounts, is discreditable. It exhibits De Quincey at about his very worst; for, though raising the estimate of Goethe's genius that had been announced in the earlier critical paper on his " Wilhelm Meister," it retains something of the malice of that paper.

When we pass to the papers of historical description, it is hardly a surprise to find that it is De Quincey's tendency in such papers to run to disputed or momentous "points" and concentrate the attention on those. A magazine paper did not afford breadth of canvas enough for complete historical representation under such titles as he generally chose. No exception of the kind, indeed, can be taken to his *Revolt of the Tartars*, which is a noble effort of historical painting, done with a sweep and breadth of poetic imagination entitling it, though a history, to rank also among his prose-phantasies. Nor does the remark apply to the *Account of the Williams Murders*, which beats for ghastly power anything else known in Newgate Calendar literature. But the tendency to "points" is shown in most of the other papers in the same sub-class. Among these *The Philosophy of Herodotus* may be mentioned for its singularly fine appreciation of the Grecian father of History, and *Modern Greece* for its amusing and humorous instructiveness. *Rhetoric* and *Style* are among De Quincey's greatest performances; and, though in them too, considered as sketches of Literary History, the strength runs towards points and specialities, the titles declare that beforehand and indicate what the specialities are. *The Cæsars* is, undoubtedly, his most ambitious attempt, all in all, in the historical department; and he set great store by it himself; but it cannot, I think, take rank among his highest productions. There are striking passages and suggestions in it; but the general effect is too hazy, many of the parts are hurried, and none of the characters of the Emperors stands out with convincing distinctness after that of Julius Cæsar.

Few authors are so difficult to represent by mere extracts as De Quincey, so seldom does he complete a matter within a short space. The following, however, may pass as specimens of him in the descriptive and historical department. The second is excellent and memorable :—

### First Sight of Dr. Parr.

Nobody announced him; and we were left to collect his name from his dress and his conversation. Hence it happened that for some time I was disposed to question with myself whether this might not be Mr. Bobus even (little as it could be supposed to resemble *him*), rather than Dr. Parr, so much did he contradict all my rational preconceptions. "A man," said I, "who has insulted people so outrageously ought not to have done this in single reliance upon his professional protections : a brave man, and a man of honour, would here have carried about with him, in his manner and deportment, some such language as this,—— ' Do not think that I shelter myself under my gown from the natural consequences of the affronts I offer : mortal combats I am forbidden, sir, as a Christian minister, to engage in ; but, as I find it impossible to refrain from occasional licence of tongue, I am very willing to fight a few rounds in a ring with any gentleman who fancies himself ill-used.' " Let me not be misunderstood ; I do not contend that Dr. Parr should often, or regularly, have offered this species of satisfaction. But I *do* insist upon it,—that no man should have given the very highest sort of provocation so wantonly as Dr. Parr is recorded to have done, unless conscious that, in a last extremity, he was ready, like a brave man, to undertake a short turn-up, in a private room, with any person whatsoever whom he had insulted past endurance. A doctor who had so often tempted (which is a kind way of saying had *merited*) a cudgelling ought himself to have had some ability to cudgel. Dr. Johnson assuredly would have acted on that principle. Had volume the second of that same folio with which he floored Osburn happened to lie ready to the prostrate man's grasp, nobody can suppose that Johnson would have disputed Osburn's right to retaliate ; in which case a regular succession of rounds would have been established. Considerations such as these, and Dr. Parr's undeniable reputation (granted even by his most admiring biographers) as a sanguinary flagellator through his long career of pedagogue, had prepared me,—nay, entitled me,—to expect in Dr. Parr a huge carcase of a man, fourteen stone at the least. Hence, then, my surprise, and the perplexity I have recorded, when the door opened, and a little man, in a most plebeian wig, . . . cut his way through the company, and made for a *fauteuil* standing opposite the fire. Into this he *lunged* ; and then forthwith, without preface or apology, began to open his talk upon the room. Here arose a new marvel, and a greater. If I had been scandalized at Dr. Parr's want of thews and bulk, conditions so indispensable for enacting the part of Sam Johnson, much more, and with better reason, was I now petrified with his voice, utterance, gestures, demeanour. Conceive, reader,

by way of counterpoise to the fine classical pronunciation of Dr.
Johnson, an infantine lisp,—the worst I ever heard,—from the
lips of a man above sixty, and accompanied with all sorts of
ridiculous grimaces and little stage gesticulations. As he sat
in his chair, turning alternately to the right and to the left,
that he might distribute his edification in equal proportions
amongst us, he seemed the very image of a little French
gossiping abbé. Yet all that I have mentioned was, and seemed
to be, a trifle by comparison with the infinite pettiness of his
matter. Nothing did he utter but little shreds of calumnious
tattle, the most ineffably silly and frivolous of all that was then
circulating in the Whig *salons* of London against the Regent.
. . . He began precisely in these words : " Oh ! I shall tell you"
(laying a stress upon the word *shall*, which still further aided
the resemblance to a Frenchman) "a sto-hee" (lispingly for
story) "about the Pince Wegent" (such was his nearest ap-
proximation to *Prince Regent*). "Oh, the Pince Wegent!—
the Pince Wegent!—what a sad Pince Wegent!" And so
the old babbler went on, sometimes wringing his hands in
lamentation, sometimes flourishing them with French grimaces
and shrugs of shoulders, sometimes expanding and contracting
his fingers like a fan. After an hour's twaddle of this scan-
dalous description, suddenly he rose, and hopped out of the
room, exclaiming all the way " *Oh, what a Pince !—Oh,
what a Wegent ! Is it a Wegent, is it a Pince, that you call
this man ? Oh, what a sad Pince ! Did anybody ever
hear of such a sad Pince !—such a sad Wegent—such a sad,
sad Pince Wegent ? Oh, what a Pince !*" &c., *da capo*. Not
without indignation did I exclaim to myself, on this winding
up of the scene, "And so this, then, this lithping slander-
monger, and retailer of gossip fit rather for washerwomen
over their tea than for scholars and statesmen, is the champion
whom his party would propound as the adequate antagonist
of Samuel Johnson ! Faugh !" . . . . Such was my first interview with Dr. Parr ; such its issue. And now let me explain
my drift in thus detailing its circumstances. Some people will
say the drift was doubtless to exhibit Dr. Parr in a dis-
advantageous light,—as a petty gossiper and a man of mean

personal appearance. No, by no means. Far from it. I, that write this paper, have myself a mean personal appearance; and I love men of mean appearance. . . . Dr. Parr, therefore, lost nothing in *my* esteem by showing a meanish exterior. Yet even this was worth mentioning, and had a value in reference to my present purpose. I like Dr. Parr; I may say even that I *love* him, for some noble qualities of heart that really did belong to him, and were continually breaking out in the midst of his singular infirmities. But this, or a far nobler moral character than Dr. Parr's, can offer no excuse for giving a false elevation to his intellectual pretensions, and raising him to a level which he will be found incapable of keeping when the props of partial friendship are withdrawn.—*Works,* V. 36–43.

### SUMMARY VIEW OF THE HISTORY OF GREEK LITERATURE.

There were two groups or clusters of Grecian wits, two deposits or stratifications of the national genius; and these were about a century apart. What makes them specially rememberable is the fact that each of these brilliant clusters had gathered separately about that man as their central pivot who, even apart from this relation to the literature, was otherwise the leading spirit, of his age. . . . Who were they? The one was PERICLES, the other was ALEXANDER OF MACEDON. Except Themistocles, who may be ranked as senior to Pericles by one generation (or thirty-three years), in the whole deduction of Grecian annals no other public man, statesman, captain-general, administrator of the national resources, can be mentioned as approaching to these two men in splendour of reputation, or  even in real merit. Pisistratus was too far back; Alcibiades, who might (chronologically speaking) have been the son of Pericles, was too unsteady and (according to Mr. Coleridge's coinage) "unreliable," or perhaps, in more correct English, too "*unrelyuponable.*" Thus far our purpose prospers. No man can pretend to forget two such centres as Pericles for the elder group, or Alexander of Macedon (the "strong he-goat" of Jewish prophecy) for the junior. Round these two *foci,* in two different but adjacent centuries, gathered the total starry

heavens, the galaxy, the Pantheon of Grecian intellect. . . .
That we may still more severely search the relations in all
points between the two systems, let us assign the chronological
*locus* of each, because that will furnish another element
towards the exact distribution of the chart representing the
motion and the oscillations of human genius. Pericles had a
very long administration. He was Prime Minister of Athens
for upwards of one entire generation. He died in the year
429 before Christ, and in a very early stage of that great
Peloponnesian war which was the one sole intestine war for
Greece, affecting *every* nook and angle in the land. Now, in
this long public life of Pericles, we are at liberty to fix on *any*
year as his chronological *locus*. On good reasons, not called for
in this place, we fix on the year 444 before Christ. This is too
remarkable to be forgotten. *Four, four, four,* what in some
games of cards is called a "*prial*" (we presume, by an elision of
the first vowel, for *parial*), forms an era which no man can
forget. It was the fifteenth year before the death of Pericles,
and not far from the bisecting year of his political life. Now,
passing to the other system, the *locus* of Alexander is quite as
remarkable, as little liable to be forgotten when once indicated,
and more easily determined, because selected from a narrower
range of choice. The exact chronological *locus* of Alexander is
333 years before Christ. Everybody knows how brief was the
career of this great man : it terminated in the year 323 before
Christ. But the *annus mirabilis* of his public life, the most
effective and productive year throughout his oriental anabasis,
was the year 333 before Christ. Here we have another "*prial,*"
a prial of threes, for the *locus* of Alexander, if properly corrected. Thus far the elements are settled, the chronological
longitude and latitude of the two great planetary systems into
which the Greek literature breaks up and distributes itself :
444 and 333 are the two central years for the two systems ;
allowing, therefore, an interspace of 111 years between the *foci*
of each. . . . Passing onwards from Pericles, you find that all
the rest in *his* system were men in the highest sense creative,
absolutely setting the very first example, each in his particular
walk of composition ; themselves without previous models, and

yet destined every man of them to become models for all after-generations; themselves without fathers or mothers, and yet having all posterity for their children. First come the three men *divini spiritus*, under a heavenly afflatus, Æschylus, Sophocles, Euripides, the creators of Tragedy out of a village mummery; next comes Aristophanes, who breathed the breath of life into Comedy; then comes the great philosopher, Anaxagoras, who first theorized successfully on man and the world. Next come, whether great or not, the still more *famous* philosophers, Socrates, Plato, Xenophon; then comes, leaning upon Pericles, as sometimes Pericles leaned upon *him*, the divine artist, Phidias; and behind this immortal man walk Herodotus and Thucydides. What a procession to Eleusis would these men have formed! what a frieze, if some great artist could arrange it as dramatically as Chaucer has arranged the Pilgrimage to Canterbury! . . . Now, let us step on a hundred years forward. We are now within hail of Alexander, and a brilliant consistory of Grecian men that is by which *he* is surrounded. There are now exquisite masters of the more refined comedy; there are, again, great philosophers, for all the great schools are represented by able successors; and, above all others, there is the one philosopher who played with men's minds (according to Lord Bacon's comparison) as freely as ever his princely pupil with their persons,—there is Aristotle. There are great orators; and, above all others, there is that orator whom succeeding generations (wisely or not) have adopted as the representative name for what is conceivable as oratorical perfection,—there is Demosthenes. Aristotle and Demosthenes are in themselves bulwarks of power; many hosts lie in those two names. For artists, again, to range against Phidias, there is Lysippus the sculptor, and there is Apelles the painter; for great captains and masters of strategic art, there is Alexander himself, with a glittering *cortége* of general officers, well qualified to wear the crowns which they will win, and to head the dynasties which they will found. Historians there are now, as in that former age; and, upon the whole, it cannot be denied that the "turn-out" is showy and imposing. . . . Before comparing the second "deposit" (geologically speaking) of Grecian genius with the

first, let us consider what it was (if anything) that connected
them.   Here, reader, we would wish to put a question.   Saving
your presence, Did you ever see what is called a dumb-bell?
*We* have ; and know it by more painful evidence than that of
sight.   You, therefore, O reader! if personally cognisant of
dumb-bells, we will remind, if not, we will inform, that it is a
cylindrical bar of iron or lead, issuing at each end in a globe of
the same metal, and usually it is sheathed in green baize. . . .
Now, reader, it is under this image of the dumb-bell that we
couch our allegory.   Those globes at each end are the two
systems or separate clusters of Greek literature ; and that
cylinder which connects them is the long man that ran into each
system, binding the two together.   Who was that?   It was
Isocrates.   *Great* we cannot call him in conscience ; and therefore, by way of compromise, we call him *long,* which, in one
sense, he certainly was; for he lived through four-and-twenty
Olympiads, each containing four solar years.   He narrowly
escaped being a hundred years old; and, though that did not
carry him from centre to centre, yet, as each system might be
supposed to protend a radius each way of twenty years, he had,
in fact, a full personal cognisance (and pretty equally) of the
two systems, remote as they were, which composed the total
world of Grecian genius. . . .  Now then, reader, you have
arrived at that station from which you overlook the whole of
Greek literature, as a few explanations will soon convince you.
Where is Homer?  where is Hesiod?  you ask ; where is
Pindar?   Homer and Hesiod lived 1000 years B.C., or, by the
lowest computation, near 900.   For anything that we know, they
may have lived with Tubal Cain.   At all events, they belong to
no power or agency that set in motion the age of Pericles, or that
operated on that age.   Pindar, again, was a solitary emanation
of some unknown influences, at Thebes, more than five hundred
years before Christ.   He may be referred to the same age as
Pythagoras.   These are all that can be cited *before* Pericles.
Next, for the ages *after* Alexander, it is certain that Greece
Proper was so much broken in spirit by the loss of her autonomy,
dating from that era, as never again to have rallied sufficiently
to produce a single man of genius,—not one solitary writer who

acted as a power upon the national mind. Callimachus was
nobody, and not decidedly Grecian. Theocritus, a man of real
genius in a limited way, is a Grecian in that sense only according to which an Anglo-American is an Englishman.
Besides that, one swallow does not make a summer. Of any
other writers, above all others of Menander, apparently a man
of divine genius, we possess only a few wrecks; and of
Anacreon, who must have been a poet of original power, we do
not certainly know that we have even any wrecks. Of those
which pass under his name not merely the authorship, but the
era, is very questionable indeed. Plutarch and Lucian, the
unlearned reader must understand, both belong to post-Christian
ages. And, for all the Greek emigrants who may have written
histories, such as we now value for their matter more than for
their execution, one and all, they belong too much to Roman
civilization that we should ever think of connecting them with
native Greek literature. Polybius in the days of the second
Scipio, Dion Cassius and Appian in the acmé of Roman civility,
are no more Grecian authors because they wrote in Greek than
the Emperors Marcus Antoninus and Julian were other than
Romans because, from monstrous coxcombry, they chose to
write in Greek their barren memoranda.—*Works*, X. 242-255.

It would be hopeless to seek to represent by extracts,
even in this inadequate fashion, that very characteristic
portion of De Quincey's writings of the generally historical
kind which we have called his Historical Speculations and
Researches. They must be read in their integrity. *The
Casuistry of Roman Meals, Cicero, Judas Iscariot, The
Essenes*, and *The Pagan Oracles*, may be especially recommended. They are admirable specimens of his boldness
and acuteness in questioning received historical beliefs,
and of his ingenuity in working out novelties or paradoxes.
The drift of *The Casuistry of Roman Meals* is that the
Romans, and indeed the ancients generally, had no such
regular meal early in the day as our modern breakfast,
and that a whole coil of important social conse-

quences depended on that one fact. In his *Cicero* he propounds a view of his own as to the character of the famous Roman orator and wit and his function in the struggle between Cæsar and Pompey. The paradox in *Judas Iscariot* is that Judas was not the vulgar traitor of the popular conception, but a headstrong fanatic, who, having missed the true spiritual purport of Christ's mission, and attached himself to Christ in the expectation of a political revolution to be effected by Christ's assumption of a temporal kingship or championship of the Jewish race, had determined to precipitate matters by leaving Christ no room for hesitation or delay. In *The Essenes* the attempt is to show that there was no real or independent sect of that name among the Jews, all the confusion to the contrary having originated in a rascally invention of the historian Josephus. In *The Pagan Oracles* there is a contradiction of the tradition of a sudden paralysis of the Pagan ritual on the first appearance of Christianity, and a castigation of the early Christian writers for having invented the pious lie.

## II. SPECULATIVE, DIDACTIC, AND CRITICAL.

While a speculative and critical element is discernible in almost all the papers now dismissed as in the main biographical or historical, and while some of the historical papers were regarded by De Quincey himself as typical examples of the speculative essay, it is of a different set of his papers that our classification obliges us to take account under the present heading. They also fall into subdivisions:—

I. METAPHYSICAL, PSYCHOLOGICAL, AND ETHICAL:—In this subdivision, itself composite, but answering to what passes under the name of PHILOSOPHY in a general sense, may be included the following:—*System of the Heavens as revealed by Lord Rosse's Telescopes;* various papers or portions of papers relating to Kant, e. g. part of the *Letters to a Young Man whose Education has been neglected,* the paper entitled *Kant in his Miscellaneous Essays,* and the translation of Kant's *Idea of a Universal History on a Cosmopolitical Plan;* the scraps entitled *Dreaming* and *The Palimpsest of the Human Brain,* in the "Sequel to the Confessions of an English Opium-Eater" (Vol. XVI.); some of the scraps in the "Notes from the Pocket-Book of a Late Opium-Eater," e. g. *On Suicide;* and the articles entitled *Plato's Republic, Glance at the Works of Mackintosh, Casuistry, On War, National Temperance Movements, Presence of Mind,* and *The Juggernaut of Social Life.*

II. THEOLOGICAL :—*Protestantism, Miracles as Subjects of Testimony, On Christianity as an Organ of Political Movement,* and *Memorial Chronology on a new and more apprehensible system.* This last, included in Vol. XVI., is an unfinished paper, posthumously published from the author's manuscript; and it contains little more than a clever and humorous introduction, in the form of an address to a young lady, with the beginning of what was intended to be a piece of Biblical Criticism.

III. ENGLISH POLITICS :—*A Tory's Account of Toryism, Whiggism, and Radicalism; On the Political Parties of Modern England; Falsification of English History.*

IV. POLITICAL ECONOMY :—*Logic of Political Economy; Dialogues of Three Templars on Political Economy;* the scraps entitled *Malthus* and *Measure of Value* in the "Notes from the Pocket-Book of a Late Opium-Eater"; and the article entitled *California.*

V. LITERARY THEORY AND CRITICISM :—The large essays entitled *Rhetoric* and *Style* may be here noted again; and there may be associated with them, as expositions of general literary theory, the *Letters to a Young Man whose Education has been neglected,* and the article entitled *Language* (which, despite the title, is really on Style). The more special articles of the same sort form a numerous series. Arranged in the

chronological order of their subjects, they are as follows:—
*Theory of Greek Tragedy, The Antigone of Sophocles,* and
*The Theban Sphinx; On the Knocking at the Gate in Mac-
beth;* the short critical paper entitled *Milton* (in Vol. VI.), and
the other entitled *Milton versus Southey and Landor* (in
Vol. XI.); the review entitled *Schlosser's Literary History of
the Eighteenth Century;* the two critical articles on Pope,
entitled *Alexander Pope* (in Vol. VIII.) and *Lord Carlisle on
Pope* (in Vol. XII.); the article *Oliver Goldsmith* (slightly
biographical, but chiefly critical); the paper on Carlyle's Translation of Wilhelm Meister, reprinted under the title *Goethe
Reflected in his Novel of Wilhelm Meister,* with omission of
the remarks on the translator (in Vol. XII.); the sketch *John
Paul Frederick Richter,* prefixed to the translated "Analects
from Richter" (in Vol. XIII.); the essay *On Wordsworth's
Poetry;* the *Notes on Godwin and Foster,* the slight little
paper entitled *John Keats,* and the *Notes on Walter Savage
Landor.* To these may be added *Orthographic Mutineers,
The Art of Conversation,* the scrap *Walladmor,* and one or
two of the scraps called " Notes from the Pocket-Book of a
Late Opium-Eater."

To the harder varieties of speculative Philosophy, it
will be observed, De Quincey has contributed less of an
original kind than might have been expected from his
known private passion for metaphysical studies. If we
except his *System of the Heavens,* which hints metaphysical ideas in the form of a splendid cosmological vision,
and his *Palimpsest of the Human Brain,* which is full of
psychological suggestion, he seems to have satisfied himself in this department by reports from Kant and recom-.
mendations of Kant to English attention. The accuracy
of some of his statements about Kant, and indeed of his
knowledge of Kant, has been called in question of late;
but it remains to his credit that, in a singularly bleak and
vapid period of the native British philosophizing, he had

contracted such an admiration, all in all, for the great
German transcendentalist. His translation of Kant's *Idea
of a Universal History* was a feat in itself. That essay
remains to this day the clearest argument for the possibility of a Science of History since Vico propounded the
*Scienza Nuova ;* and to have perceived the importance of
such an essay in the year 1824 was to be in possession of
a philosophical notion of great value long before it was
popular in Britain. That De Quincey contented himself so much with mere accounts of Kant personally, and
literary glimpses of the nature of his speculations, may
have been due to the fact that original philosophizing of
the metaphysical and psychological kinds was not wanted
in magazines and would not pay. He made amends, however, as our list will have shown, by a considerable quantity of writing on subjects of Speculative Ethics. His
best essay of this kind is that entitled *Casuistry*. It was
a favourite idea of De Quincey's that Moral Philosophy
in recent times, especially in Protestant countries, has run
too much upon generalities, avoiding too much those very
*cases* of constant recurrence in life about which difficulties
are likely to arise in practical conduct. Accordingly, in
this essay, there is a discussion of duelling and the laws
of honour, the legitimacy of suicide, proper behaviour to
servants, the limits of the rule of veracity, &c., &c., all
with lively historical illustrations. In the paper *On War*
the necessary permanence of that agency in the world is
asserted strongly, and a certain character of nobleness and
beneficence claimed for it. There is less of dissent from
current philanthropy in the article on *Temperance Movements ;* but it will not give entire satisfaction. The article
on *Plato's Republic* is a virulent attack upon a philosopher
towards whom we should have expected to see De Quincey

standing in an attitude of discipleship and veneration.  This is owing chiefly to De Quincey's disgust with
the moral heresies, in the matter of marriage and the like,
on which Plato so coolly professes to found his imaginary
commonwealth ; and it is possible that, had he been
treating Plato in respect of the sum-total of his philosophic and literary merits, we should have had a much
more admiring estimate.  As it is, one has to pity De
Quincey rather than Plato in this unfortunate interview.
He looks as petulant and small in his attack on Plato as
he did in his attack on Goethe.

The expressly theological papers of De Quincey, with
passages innumerable through his other writings, show
that he took his stand on established Christian orthodoxy.
He avowed his belief in a miraculous revelation from
God to mankind, begun and continued in the history of
the Jewish race, and consummated in the life of Christ
and in the diffusion of Christianity by the Apostles.  As
a reasoned piece of Christian apologetics his answer to
Hume's argument, entitled *Miracles as Subjects of Testimony*, does not seem to have won much regard from
theologians, and, though very subtle, is certainly deficient
in the homely quality which Hobbes called *bite*.  His
own religious faith, indeed appears to have been very
much of the nature of an inherited sentiment, independent
of reasoning, and which he would not let reasoning
disturb.  In one respect, too, his theology was of what
many theologians now would call a narrow and old-
fashioned kind.  There is no trace in him of that notion
of a universal religious inspiration among the nations, and
so of a certain respectability, greater or less, in all mytho-
logies, which has been fostered by the modern science
of religions.  On the contrary, Christianity is with him

the single divine revelation in the world, and he thinks
and speaks of the Pagan religions, in the style of the old-
fashioned theology, as simply false religions, horrid religions, inventions of the spirit of evil.   How this is to be
reconciled with his wide range of historical sympathy,
and especially with his admiration of the achievements
of the Greek intellect and the grandeur of the Roman
character, it might be difficult to say.  Probably it was
because he distinguished between those noble and admirable developments which human nature could work
out for itself, and which therefore belong to humanity as
such, and the more rare and spiritual possibilities which
he believed actual revelation had woven into the web of
humanity, and which were to be regarded as gifts from the
supernatural.  At all events, the matter stands as has
been stated.  In the same way, Mahometanism figures in
his regard as of little worth, monotheistic certainly and
therefore superior to the Pagan creeds, but a spurious
religion and partly stolen.   Further, De Quincey's Christianity declares itself as deliberately of the Protestant
species.  With much respect for Roman Catholicism, he
yet repudiates it as in great measure a corruption of the
original system, which original system he finds reproduced
in the Protestantism of the sixteenth century.  His article
entitled *Protestantism* is an exposition of his views in that
matter, and is altogether a very able and important paper.
If he has seemed narrow hitherto in his philosophy of
religion, here, once within the bounds of his Protestantism,
and engaged in defining Protestantism, he becomes broad
enough.  "The self-sufficingness of the Bible and the right
of private judgment" are, he maintains, "the two great
characters in which Protestantism commences," and the
doctrines by which it distinguishes itself from the Church

of Rome. Bound up in these doctrines, he maintains, is the duty of absolute religious toleration ; and by this principle of absolute religious toleration, the right of the individual to think, print, and publish what he pleases, he abides with exemplary fidelity through all his writings, even while in skirmish with the free-thinkers for whom he has the strongest personal disgust. But this is not all. He abjures *Bibliolatry*, or that kind of respect for the letter of the Bible which is founded on the notion of verbal inspiration, denying it to be a necessary tenet of Protestantism, or to be possible indeed for any scholarly understanding. It is not only, he maintains, that the notion of literal or verbal inspiration is broken down at once by recollection of the corruptions of the original text of the Scriptures, their various readings, and the fact that it is only in translations that the Scriptures exist for the masses of mankind in all countries. He addresses himself more emphatically to the alleged palpable errors in the substance and teachings of the Bible, its violations of history and chronology, its inconsistencies with modern science. Here he refuses at once that method of reconciling science with Scripture which proceeds by torture of texts into meanings different from those which they bore to the Hebrews or the Greeks who first read them. His bold principle is that Science and the Bible cannot be reconciled in such matters, and that the desire to reconcile them indicates a most gross and carnal misconception of the very idea of a divine revelation. The principle may be given in his own words :—

It is an obligation resting upon the Bible, if it is to be consistent with itself, that it should *refuse* to teach science ; and, if the Bible ever *had* taught any one art, science, or process of

life, it would have been asked, Is a divine mission abandoned
suddenly for a human mission? By what caprice is this one
science taught, and others not? Or these two, suppose, and
not all? But an objection even deadlier would have followed.
It is clear as is the purpose of daylight that the whole body of
the arts and sciences comprises one vast machinery for the
irritation and development of the human intellect. For this
end they exist. To see God, therefore, descending into the
arena of science, and contending, as it were, for his own prizes,
by teaching science in the Bible, would be to see him inter-
cepting from their self-evident destination (viz., man's intellectual benefit) his own problems by solving them himself.
No spectacle could more dishonour the divine idea, could more
injure man under the mask of aiding him. *The Bible must
not teach anything that man can teach himself.*

The revelation of the Old and New Testaments is to be
regarded, then, according to De Quincey, as a leaven of
truths purely moral and spiritual, sent into the world by
miracle precisely because man could never have found
them out for himself, with a careful abstinence from any
mixture of matter of ordinary knowledge in advance of
what was already existent, and therefore with an adoption of all existing historical and scientific phrases and
traditions. Hence *Bibliolatry*, in the sense of a belief in
the immaculate correctness of the language and statements
of the Bible on all subjects whatsoever, was no tenet of
genuine Christianity, secure as every Christian ought to
be that, whatever changes of conception on such subjects
as the antiquity of the human race, or the system of the
physical universe, might come with the progress of the
human intelligence, the supernatural leaven would im-
pregnate them as they came, and go on working. In this
doctrine, of which De Quincey seems to have meditated a
particular application in his unfinished papers entitled
" *Memorial Chronology*," he was substantially at one with

Coleridge and Wordsworth. He was at one with them, too, in his affection for Church-Establishments. In remarkable difference from his favourite Milton, who regarded the incorporation of Church and State as the cause of the vitiation of the supernatural leaven in the world, and scowled back with hatred on the Emperor Constantine as the beginner of that mischief, De Quincey confessed to a special kindness for Constantine, precisely because that Emperor had conceived the idea of converting Christianity into a political agency. It was Constantine who had carried Christian teaching into effect in such institutions as hospitals and public provision for the poor ; and the prospects of the world for the future were bound up with the possible extensions of the political influence of Christianity in similar directions. That is the subject of the essay entitled *On Christianity as an Organ of Political Movement*. In short, De Quincey is to be remembered, in his religious relations, as a staunch Church-of-England man of the broad school, not given to High-Church sacerdotalism, though with an æsthetic liking in his own case for a comely ritual.

In politics De Quincey was an English Tory. In the two papers entitled *A Tory's Account of Toryism, Whiggism, and Radicalism*, and *On the Political Parties of Modern England*, he avows his partisanship. Toryism asserts itself also in the article on Dr. Parr, and tinges some of the other papers. It is interesting, indeed, to observe how much of the " John Bull element," as Mr. Page calls it, there was, all in all, in the feeble little man. His patriotism was of the old type of the days of Pitt and Nelson. He exulted in the historic glories of England and her imperial ascendency in so many parts of the

globe, and would have had her do battle for any punctilio of
honour, as readily as for any more visible interest, in her
dealings with foreigners.  He had a good deal of the old
English anti-Gallican prejudice ; and, though he has done
justice, over and over again, to some of the finer characteristics of the French, the total effect of his remarks
on the French, politically and intellectually, is irritating
to the admirers of that great nation.  He knew them only
through books or by casual observation of stray French-
men he met ; for he was never out of the British Islands,
and never experienced that sudden awakening of a positive
affection for the French which comes infallibly from even
a single visit to their lightsome capital.  On the other
hand, though Scotland was his home for so large a part of
his life, he seems never to have contracted the least
sympathy with anything distinctively Scottish.  Even
his Toryism was specially English or South-British.  But,
like all other parts of his creed, his Toryism was of a
highly intellectual kind, with features of its own.  In
such questions, for example, as that of the continuance
of flogging and other brutal forms of punishment in the
army and navy and elsewhere, he parted company with
the ordinary mass of Tories, leaving his curse with them in
that particular, and went with the current of Radical
sentiment and opinion.  How far he was carried, by
his candour of intellect and depth and accuracy of scholarship, from the ordinary rut of party commonplace, may
be judged also from his little paper entitled *Falsification
of English History*.  It is a gallant little paper, and one
of the best rebukes in our language to that systematic
vilification of the Puritan Revolution, the English
Commonwealth, and the Reign of Cromwell, which has
come down in the Anglican mind as an inheritance from

the Restoration, and still vulgarises so much of our scholarship and our literature.

The *Dialogues of the Three Templars* and the *Logic of Political Economy* are De Quincey's chief contributions to the literature of Economic Science. As to the literary deftness of the essay and the treatise there is no doubt. For cutting lucidity of exposition and beauty of style they are to be envied by most writers on Political Economy. This seems to have been felt by Mr. John Stuart Mill, who mentions De Quincey with respect, and uses quotations from him thankfully, in parts of his standard work. The question rather is whether De Quincey has any title, such as he himself seemed to claim, to the character of an original thinker in the matter of the science. Mr. Mill's language in one place appears to negative this claim, though very gently ; and the question has been reopened, in De Quincey's interest, by Mr. Shadworth Hodgson in an essay entitled " De Quincey as Political Economist." Enough here on that matter.

If De Quincey surpasses himself anywhere in his didactic papers, it is in those that concern Literary Theory and Criticism. No English writer has left a finer body of disquisition on the science and principles of Literature than will be found in De Quincey's general papers entitled *Rhetoric, Style,* and *Language,* and his *Letters to a Young Man,* together with his more particular articles entitled *Theory of Greek Tragedy, The Antigone of Sophocles, Milton, Milton versus Southey and Landor, Alexander Pope, Lord Carlisle on Pope, Schlosser's Literary History of the Eighteenth Century,* and *On Wordsworth's Poetry.* There, or elsewhere in De Quincey, will be found the last word, so far as there can be a last word, on some of the most important questions of style or

literary art, and a treatment of literary questions throwing
back into mere obsolete ineptitude the literary theories of
such masters of the eighteenth century as Addison and
Johnson, and of such of their successors as the acute
Jeffrey and the robust but coarse-grained Whately.
Goethe, the greatest literary critic that ever lived, was more
comprehensive and universally tolerant ; but De Quincey
was *facile princeps*, to the extent of his touch, among
the English critics of his generation. He acknowledged
that he had received some of his leading ideas in literary
art from Wordsworth originally ; but whatever he derived
from Wordsworth was matured by so much independent
reflection, and so modified by the peculiarities of his own
temperament, that the result was a system of precepts
differing from Wordsworth's in not a few points.

One of the best known of De Quincey's critical maxims
is his distinction, after Wordsworth, between the Literature
of Knowledge, which he would call Literature only by
courtesy, and the Literature of Power, which alone he
regarded as Literature proper. My belief is that the distinction has been overworked in the form in which De
Quincey put it forth, and that it would require a great
deal of re-explication and modification to bring it into
defensible and permanent shape. As it would be unpardonable, however, to omit this De Quinceyism in a
sketch of De Quincey's opinions, here is one of the
passages in which he expounds it :—

### THE LITERATURE OF KNOWLEDGE AND THE LITERATURE OF POWER.

In that great social organ which, collectively, we call Literature,
there may be distinguished two separate offices that may blend
and often do so, but capable, severally, of a severe insulation,
and naturally fitted for reciprocal repulsion. There is, first, the

literature of *knowledge*, and, secondly, the literature of *power*. The function of the first is to *teach ;* the function of the second is to *move :* the first is a rudder, the second an oar or a sail. The first speaks to the *mere* discursive understanding ; the second speaks ultimately, it may happen, to the higher understanding or reason, but always' *through* affections of pleasure and sympathy. Remotely, it may travel towards an object seated in what Lord Bacon calls *dry* light ; but, proximately, it does and must operate, else it ceases to be a literature of *power*, in and through that *humid* light which clothes itself in the mists and glittering iris of human passions, desires, and genial emotions. Men have so little reflected on the higher functions of literature as to find it a paradox if one should describe it as a mean or subordinate purpose of books to give information. But this is a paradox only in the sense which makes it honourable to be paradoxical. Whenever we talk in ordinary language of seeking information or gaining knowledge, we understand the words as connected with something of absolute novelty. But it is the grandeur of all truth which *can* occupy a very high place in human interests that it is never absolutely novel to the meanest of minds : it exists eternally by way of germ or latent principle in the lowest as in the highest, needing to be developed, but never to be planted. To be capable of transplantation is the immediate criterion of a truth that ranges on a lower scale. Besides which, there is a rarer thing than truth,—namely, *power*, or deep sympathy with truth. . . . Were it not that human sensibilities are ventilated and continually called out into exercise by the great phenomena of infancy, or of real life as it moves through chance and change, or of literature as it recombines these elements in the mimicries of poetry, romance, &c., it is certain that, like any animal power or muscular energy falling into disuse, all such sensibilities would gradually drop and dwindle. It is in relation to these great *moral* capacities of man that the literature of power, as contradistinguished from that of knowledge, lives and has its field of action. It is concerned with what is highest in man ; for the Scriptures themselves never condescended to deal, by suggestion or co-operation, with the mere discursive understanding: when speaking of man in his intellectual capacity, the Scriptures speak not of the understanding, but of "*the understanding heart*,"—making the heart, *i. e.* the great intuitive (or non-discursive) organ, to be the interchangeable formula for man in his highest state of capacity for the infinite. Tragedy, romance, fairy tale, or epopee, all alike restore to man's mind the ideals of justice, of hope, of truth, of mercy, of retribution, which else (left to the support of daily life in its realities) would languish for want of sufficient illustration. . . . Hence the pre-eminency over all authors that merely *teach* of the meanest that *moves*, or that teaches, if at all, indirectly by moving. The very highest work that has ever existed in the literature of knowledge is but a *provisional* work, a book upon trial and sufferance, and *quamdiu bene se gesserit*. Let its teaching be even partially revised, let it be but expanded, nay, let its teaching be but placed in a better order, and instantly it is superseded. Whereas the feeblest works in the literature of power, surviving at all, survive as finished and unalterable amongst men. For instance, the *Principia* of Sir Isaac Newton was a book *militant* on earth from the first. In all stages of its progress it would have to fight for its existence,—first, as regards absolute truth; secondly, when that combat was over, as regards its form or mode of presenting the truth. And, as soon as a La Place, or anybody else, builds higher upon the founda-tions laid by this book, effectually he throws it out of the sunshine into decay and darkness; by weapons even from this book he superannuates and destroys this book, so that soon the name of Newton remains as a mere *nominis umbra*, but his book, as a living power, has transmigrated into other forms. Now, on the contrary, the *Iliad*, the *Prometheus* of Æschylus, the *Othello* or *King Lear*, the *Hamlet* or *Macbeth*, or the *Paradise Lost*, are not militant, but triumphant for ever, as long as the languages exist in which they speak or can be taught to speak. They never *can* transmigrate into new incarnations. To reproduce *them* in new forms or variations, even if in some things they should be improved, would be to plagiarize. A good steam-engine is properly super-seded by a better. But one lovely pastoral valley is not superseded by another, nor a statue of Praxiteles by a statue of Michael Angelo.—*Works*, viii. 5—9.

### III. IMAGINATIVE WRITINGS AND PROSE POETRY.

In this class may be reckoned the following :—

I. HUMOROUS EXTRAVAGANZAS :—The paragon in this kind is, of course, *Murder considered as one of the Fine Arts*. There are, however, occasional passages of frolicsome invention through the other papers ; and the entire paper *Sortilege and Astrology* may be taken as a *jeu d'esprit* of the same sort.

II. INCIDENTS OF REAL LIFE AND PASSAGES OF HISTORY TREATED IMAGINATIVELY :—In addition to the poetic versions of incidents from real life that are interwrought with the expressly autobiographic writings, there ought to be mentioned specially the paper entitled *Early Memorials of Grasmere*. It is the story of the loss of two peasants, a husband and his wife, among the hills, during a snowstorm in the Lake District, in the year 1807. In the same group, on grounds of literary principle, may be reckoned the story called *The Spanish Military Nun* and the paper entitled *Joan of Arc*. As has been already hinted, *The Revolt of the Tartars* might rank in the same high company.

III. NOVELETTES AND ROMANCES :—Chief among these is De Quincey's one-volume novel or romance, *Klosterheim*, published in 1832, and unfortunately not included in the edition of his collected works, nor accessible at present in any form, to any of her Majesty's subjects, except by importation of an American reprint. In connexion with this independent attempt in prose-fiction, we may remember the short story or novelette called *The Avenger* (reprinted in vol. xvi. from *Blackwood's Magazine* of 1838) and *Walladmor*, the pseudo-Waverley Novel of 1824, which De Quincey translated from the German. There are, besides, some novelettes from the German, reprinted in the collective edition.

IV. PROSE PHANTASIES AND LYRICS :—Although De Quincey ranked the whole of his *Confessions* as properly an example of that " mode of impassioned prose " in which he thought there had been few or no precedents in English, it is enough here to

remember those parts of the *Confessions* which may be distinguished as " dream phantasies." To be added, under our
present heading (besides passages in the *Autobiographic
Sketches*), are *The Daughter of Lebanon*, the extraordinary
paper in three parts called *The English Mail Coach*, and the
little cluster of fragments called *Suspiria de Profundis* (i. e.,
" Sighs from the Depths "), *being a Sequel to the Confessions
of an English Opium-Eater*. In fact, however, only three of
the six fragments there gathered under the common name of
" Suspiria " are either " lyrics " or " phantasies," the rest being
critical or psychological. The three entitled to a place here are
those entitled *Levana and our Ladies of Sorrow, Savannah-
la-Mar*, and *Memorial Suspiria*.

The celebrity of the essay *On Murder considered as
one of the Fine Arts* is not surprising. The ghastly
originality of the conception, the humorous irony with
which it is sustained by stroke after stroke, and the mad
frenzy of the closing scene, where the assembled club
of amateurs in murder, with Toad-in-the-hole leading
them, drink their toasts and sing their chorus in honour
of certain superlative specimens of their favourite art,
leave an impression altogether exceptional, as of pleasure
mixed illegitimately with the forbidden and horrible.
For a lighter and more genial specimen of De Quincey
in his whimsical vein, *Sortilege and Astrology* may
be cordially recommended. To pass from such papers
to *Early Memorials of Grasmere*, *The Spanish Military Nun*, and *Joan of Arc*, gives one a fresh idea
of the versatility of his powers. The first, describing
winter among the English Lakes, and telling the tragic
story of George and Sarah Green, and of the bravery
of their little girl left in charge of the cottage to
which they were never to return alive, has all the
mournful beauty of a commemorative prose-poem. The

second, which is a narrative, from historical materials, of the adventures of a daring Spanish girl, in man's disguise, first in Spain and then in the Spanish parts of the new world, in the beginning of the seventeenth century, is in De Quincey's most characteristic style of mingled humour and earnestness, and has all the fascination of one of the best of the Spanish *picaresque* romances. The paper on Joan of Arc, though brief, is nobly perfect. " What is to be thought of *her ?* What " is to be thought of the poor shepherd girl from the hills " and forests of Lorraine, that, like the Hebrew shepherd " boy from the hills and forests of Judea, rose suddenly " out of the quiet, out of the safety, out of the religious " inspiration, rooted in deep pastoral solitudes, to a station " in the van of armies, and to the more perilous station at " the right hand of kings ?" Opening in this strain of poetic solemnity, the paper maintains the same high tone throughout ; and, if it does not leave the question answered by enshrining the image of the Maid of Orleans in a sufficient vision of glory, there is no such answer in the English language.

De Quincey included in his collected works two short tales of clever humour, called *The Incognito, or Count Fitzhum,* and *The King of Hayti,* and a third, called *The Dice,* a short story of devilry and black art, describing the first as " translated from the German of Dr. Schultze," and the other two merely as " from the German." Passing these and a fourth tale, called *The Fatal Marksman,* which is somewhat in the style of the third, and seems also to be from the German (though that is not stated), we have, as the single original novelette of De Quincey among the collected works, the strange piece called *The Avenger.* It is a story, wholly fantastic and

sensational, but quite in De Quincey's vein, of a series of
appalling and mysterious murders supposed to happen in
a German town in the year 1816, and of the astounding
discovery at last that they have all been the work of a certain magnificent youth, Maximilian Wyndham, of mixed
English and Jewish descent, and of immense wealth, who
had come to reside in the town, in the house of one of
the University professors, with high Russian credentials
and universal acceptance among the citizens.   He had
come thither nominally to complete his studies, but really
in pursuit of a secret scheme of vengeance upon those of
the inhabitants who had been concerned in certain deadly
injuries and dishonours done to his family, and especially
to his Jewish mother.   The story does not appear to have
been much read ; and admirers of De Quincey may judge
from this description of it whether it is worth looking
up.   It may be even more necessary to give some account
of *Klosterheim, or the Masque.*

As originally published by Blackwood in 1832, it was
a small prettily-printed volume of 305 pages, without De
Quincey's name after the title, but only the words "By
the English Opium-Eater."   It would make about half a
volume in the collective edition of the works, were it
included there.

The scene of the story is an imaginary German city,
Klosterheim, with its forest-neighbourhood ; and the time
is the winter of 1633, with part of the year 1634, or just
at that point of the great Thirty Years' War when, after the
death of Gustavus-Adolphus, his Swedish generals are
maintaining the war against the Imperialists, and all
Germany is in confusion and misery with the marchings
and counter-marchings, the ravagings and counter-ravagings,
of the opposed armies.   The Klosterheimers, as good

Catholics, are mainly in sympathy with the Imperialists, but are in the peculiar predicament of being subject to a gloomy and tyrannical Landgrave, who, though a bigoted Roman Catholic, has reasons of his own for cultivating the Swedish alliance, and is in fact in correspondence with the Swedes. A leading spirit among them, and especially among the University students, is a certain splendid soldier-youth, Maximilian, a stranger from a distance. So, when the Klosterheimers are in excitement over the approach to their city, through the forest, of a travelling mass of pilgrims, under Imperialist convoy, all the way from Vienna, and over the chances that the poor pilgrims may be attacked and cut to pieces by a certain brutal Holkerstein, the head of a host of marauders who prowl through the forest, who but this Maximilian is the man to execute the general desire of Klosterheim by evading the orders of the cruel Landgrave and carrying armed aid to the pilgrims? Well that he has done so; for in the midst of the pilgrim-cavalcade, and the chief personage in it, is his own lady-love, the noble Paulina, a relative of the Emperor, and entrusted by him with despatches. The lovers meet; and, save for a night-alarm, in the course of which the portmanteau of secret despatches is abstracted by robbers from Lady Paulina's carriage, there is no accident till the pilgrims are close to Klosterheim. There, in the night-time, Holkerstein and his host of marauders do fall upon them. There is a dreadful night-battle; and, though the marauding host is beaten off, chiefly by the heroic valour of Maximilian, it is but a wreck of the pilgrim-army that enters Klosterheim on the morrow,—and then alas! without Maximilian among them. He has been carried away by the marauders, a wounded prisoner. The residue of the poor pilgrims are dispersed through the city somehow for hospitality,

and the doleful Lady Paulina takes up her abode in the
great abbey, close to the Landgrave's palace. Then, for
a while, we are among the Klosterheimers, and called
upon to pity them. For the gloomy Landgrave, always a
tyrant, now revels in acts of tyranny and cruelty utterly
indiscriminate and capricious, maddened by the goad of
some new motive, which is not explained, but which we
connect with intelligence he has obtained from the abstracted imperial despatches. There are arrests of students
and citizens ; all are in consternation ; no one knows what
will happen next. Suddenly, however, a counter-agency
is at work in Klosterheim, baffling and bewildering the
Landgrave and his wily Italian minister Adorni. This is
a certain mysterious being, whether human or supernatural
no one can tell, who calls himself " The Masque," and
seems omnipresent and resistless. He appears when and
where he likes, passes through bolts and bars, leaves
messages to the Landgrave nailed up in public places, and
defies his police. Houses are entered ; citizens disappear,
sometimes with signs of scuffle and bloodshed left in
their rooms ; and, as these victims of "The Masque" are
not exclusively from the ranks of the Landgrave's par-
tisans, it becomes doubtful whether the mysterious being
has any political purpose, or is a mere demon of general
malignity. But, evidently, the Landgrave is his main
mark ; and it is in the palace of the Landgrave that he
makes his presence and his power most daringly felt.
How, for example, he appeared there at a great masked
ball, to which exactly twelve hundred persons had been
invited by numbered tickets ; how, when the twelve
hundred had been, by arrangement, counted off in the
hall, and aggregated apart, he was seen in majestic and
solitary composure, leaning against a marble column, and

it seemed as if the Landgrave and Adorni had but to
give the word to their myrmidons to clutch him; but
how there was nothing of that expected catastrophe, but
only a scornful disappearance of the awful figure, as if in
cloud or smoke, after some words from his hollow voice
which left the Landgrave trembling :—for all this, and
much more, there must be application inside the little
volume itself.    In reading it, you are as if in the heart of
one of Mrs. Radcliffe's novels, with the usual para-
phernalia of cloaks, nodding plumes, ghostly sounds,
labyrinthine corridors and secret passages, pictures of
ancestors on the walls, and the rest of it; and you long to
be out of such a curiosity-shop of jumbled incredibilities,
and to know the *dénouement*.    That does not come till
after new episodes of danger to Lady Paulina, new coils
of marvel round the mysterious " Masque," and a second
great assembly in the palace, with a vast mechanism of
new preparations by the infuriated Landgrave for the dis-
comfiture of his adversary.    Let these be supposed ; and
let it be supposed that the 6th of September, 1634, has
passed, and that the Swedes have been routed and the
Imperialists triumphant in the great battle of Nördlingen.
What need then for further mystery ?    The hour has
come for that revolution in Klosterheim which the Emperor himself had devised from Vienna, and manipulated
in the secret despatches he had sent by the Lady Paulina.
All is revealed in a crash.    Maximilian is the true Landgrave, the hitherto undivulged son of the last good Landgrave ; and the present usurper had come to his power by
the murder of Maximilian's father, and maintained it by
other crimes.    In the crash of this revelation the gloomy
usurper sinks, the last blow to the wretched man being
the death of his daughter by a mistake of his own murderous

order for the execution of the Lady Paulina. Maximilian
marries Paulina ; there are other more minute solutions
and surprises ; and the Klosterheimers, under their new
Landgrave, are again a happy people. But who was
the mysterious "Masque"? Who but Maximilian himself? Trap-doors and subterranean passages, his own
dexterity, and collusion with the requisite number of
citizens and students, and with an old seneschal of the
tyrant, had done the whole business ; and the only blood
really shed in the course of it had been that of the poor
seneschal, betrayed by accident, and stabbed by his
master.

Such is De Quincey's one-volume romance, a poor
performance, doubtless for the sake of a little money,
about the time when he settled in Edinburgh. Was
he ashamed of it afterwards, that he did not reprint
it? There was no necessity for that ; for, though the
story does not show the craft of a Sir Walter Scott, it is
by no means bad of its preposterous kind. The style, at
all events, is remarkably careful, with a marble beauty of
sentence that makes one linger as one reads.

There remains to be noticed, in the last place, that very
special portion of De Quincey's writings of the imaginative order for which he claimed distinction above the
rest, as illustrating "a mode of impassioned prose" but
slightly represented before in English Literature. It
may be questioned, however, whether the pieces for which
he claimed this distinction are described most exactly by
the phrase "impassioned prose." Their peculiarity is
not so much that they are impassioned in any ordinary sense as that they are imaginative or poetical
after a very definite and rather rare sort. It was one of
the distinctions of De Quincey's intellect that it could

pass from that ordinary or discursive exercise of itself
which consists in expounding, reasoning, or investigating,
to that poetic exercise of itself which consists in the
formation of visions or phantasies ; and it did, in fact, so
pass on those occasions more particularly when it was
moved by pathos or by the feeling of the mysterious and
awful. What is most observable, therefore, in the pieces
under notice is that they exhibit the operation of those
two constitutional kinds of emotion upon De Quincey's
*intellectual* activity, transmuting it from the common or
discursive mode to that called poetic imagination. Inasmuch as it is the implicated feeling or sentiment that
moves the intellectual process, and inasmuch as there are
marks of this in the rhythmical or lyrical character of the
result, there is no great harm in calling that result impassioned prose, especially if we keep to the limitation
stipulated by De Quincey's own phrase, "*a mode of* impassioned prose" ; but it is better, all in all, to define the
writings under consideration as examples of a peculiar
" mode of imaginative prose," and, if further definition is
wanted of this peculiar mode of prose poetry, to call it
*Prose Phantasy and Lyric*, or *Lyrical Prose Phantasy*. De
Quincey was consciously and deliberately an artist in this
form of prose-poetry, and has left specimens of it that
have very few parallels in English. One ought to remember, however, how much he must have been influenced
by the previous example of Jean Paul Richter. Of his
admiration of the famous German before he had himself
begun his career of literature there is proof in his article
on Richter published in the *London Magazine* in December 1821, just after the appearance of his *Confessions* in
their first form in the same Magazine; and one observes
that among the translated "analects" from Richter which

accompanied or followed that article, and were intended
to introduce Richter to the English public, were *The
Happy Life of a Parish Priest in Sweden* and the
*Dream upon the Universe*, both of them specimens of
Richter's peculiar art of prose-phantasy.   There can be no
doubt that Richter's example in such pieces influenced
De Quincey permanently.   But, though he may have learnt
something from Richter, he was an original master in the
same art.

One might go back here on his *Joan of Arc*, and some of
the other writings of which account has been already
taken, and claim for them, or for parts of them, fresh
recognition in our present connexion.   But let us confine
ourselves to the writings to which De Quincey seems to
have pointed more especially, and which have been already
enumerated.

To the famous passages of "dream-phantasy" in the
*Opium Confessions* we need not re-advert farther than to
say that, extraordinary as they are as a whole, one may
fairly object to parts of them, as to some of the similar
dream-phantasies in Richter, that they fail by too much
obtrusion of artistic self-consciousness in their construction,
and sometimes also by a swooning of the power of clear
and consecutive vision in a mere piling and excess of
imagery and sound.   The stroke on the mind at the time
is not always equal to the look of the apparatus for inflict-
ing it; and the memory does not retain a sufficient scar.
No such objection can be urged against *The Daughter of
Lebanon*, a fine visionary lyric of seven pages, figuring an
early and miraculous conversion to Christianity in the
person of an ideal girl of Damascus.   Nor would any of
De Quincey's readers give up the first two sections of
*The English Mail Coach*, subtitled "The Glory of

Motion" and "The Vision of Sudden Death." There is nothing in Jean Paul quite like these.

In the first we are back in the old days between Trafalgar and Waterloo. Drawn up at the General Post Office in Lombard Street, and waiting for the hour to start, we see His Majesty's mails,—carriages, harness, horses, lamps, the dresses of driver and guard, all in the perfection of English equipment, and, if there has been news that day of a great victory, then the laurels, the oak leaves, the flowers, the ribbons, in addition. Seating ourselves beside the driver on one of the mails, we begin our journey of three hundred miles along one of the great roads, north or west, leaving Lombard Street at a quarter past eight in the evening. How, once out into the country, we shoot along, horses at gallop, the breeze in our faces, hedges and trees and fields and homesteads rushing past us in the darkness which we and our lamps are cleaving like a fiery arrow! How, at every stopping-station, there are the lights and bustle at the inn-door, and the laurels and other bedizenments we carry are seen ere we have well stopped, and we shout " Badajoz" or " Salamanca" in explanation, or whatever else may have been the last victory, and the hostlers and other inn-folk take up the huzza, and it is one round of congratulation and hand-shaking while we stay! But, punctually to the minute, having changed horses, and left the news palpitating in that neighbourhood, we are on again, horses at gallop, coach-lamps burning, and we beside the driver on the front seat, conscious that we are carrying the same news with us to neighbourhoods still ahead! On, on, stage after stage, in the same fashion, still cleaving the darkness, the horse-hoofs always audible and the coach-lamps always burning, till the darkness yields to a silver

glimmer and the glimmer to the glare of day!—Such is
the series of sensations De Quincey has contrived to give
us in his prose-poem called "The Glory of Motion." In
the sequel, entitled "The Vision of Sudden Death,"
we are still on the same night journey by coach, or rather
on one later night journey on the northern road between
sixty and seventy years ago, with the difference that the
glory of motion is now turned into horror. Prosaically
described, the paper is a recollection of a fatal accident by
collision of the mail, in a very dark part of the road, with a
solitary vehicle containing two persons, one of them a
woman; but it is for the paper itself to show what the
incident becomes in De Quincey's hands.—It passes into
a third paper, still under the same general title of *The
English Mail Coach;* which third paper, indeed, bears the
extraordinary subtitle of "Dream-Fugue, founded on the
preceding theme of Sudden Death." I cannot say that
this "dream-fugue," which is offered as a lyrical finale to
the little series, in visionary coherence with the preceding
pieces, accomplishes its purpose very successfully. It is
liable to the objection which may be urged, as we have
said, against other specimens of De Quincey in the peculiar
art of dream-phantasy. The artifice is too apparent, and
the meaning is all but lost in a mere vague of music.

Of the three scraps of the *Suspiria* that are entitled
to rank among the lyrical prose-phantasies, viz., *Levana
and Our Ladies of Sorrow, Savannah-la-Mar,* and *Memorial
Suspiria,* only the first is of much importance. But that
scrap, written in De Quincey's later life, is of as high
importance as anything he ever wrote. It is perhaps the
highest and finest thing, and also the most constitutionally
significant, in all De Quincey. Fortunately, the essential
core of it can be quoted entire. All that it is necessary

to premise is that "Levana" was the Roman Goddess of Education, the divinity who was supposed to "lift up" every newly-born human being from the earth in token that it should live, and to rule the influences to which it should be subject thenceforth till its character should be fully formed :—

### The Three Ladies of Sorrow.

I know them thoroughly, and have walked in all their kingdoms. Three sisters they are, of one mysterious household; and their paths are wide apart; but of their dominion there is no end. Them I saw often conversing with Levana, and sometimes about myself. Do they talk, then? O, no! Mighty phantoms like these disdain the infirmities of language. They may utter voices through the organs of man when they dwell in human hearts, but amongst themselves there is no voice nor sound; eternal silence reigns in *their* kingdoms. They spoke not, as they talked with Levana; they whispered not; they sang not; though oftentimes methought they *might* have sung: for I upon earth had heard their mysteries oftentimes deciphered by harp and timbrel, by dulcimer and organ. Like God, whose servants they are, they utter their pleasure, not by sounds that perish, or by words that go astray, but by signs in heaven, by changes on earth, by pulses in secret rivers, heraldries painted in darkness, and hieroglyphics written on the tablets of the brain. *They* wheeled in mazes; *I* spelled the steps. *They* telegraphed from afar; *I* read the signals. *They* conspired together; and on the mirrors of darkness *my* eye traced the plots. *Theirs* were the symbols; *mine* are the words.

What is it the sisters are? What is it that they do? Let me describe their form and their presence: if form it were that still fluctuated in its outline, or presence it were that for ever advanced to the front or for ever receded amongst shades.

The eldest of the three is named *Mater Lachrymarum*, Our Lady of Tears. She it is that night and day raves and moans, calling for vanished faces. She stood in Rama, where a voice was heard of lamentation,—Rachel weeping for her children, and refusing to be comforted. She it was that stood in Bethlehem on the night when Herod's sword swept its nurseries of innocents, and the little feet were stiffened for ever, which, heard at times as they tottered along floors overhead, woke pulses of love in household hearts that were not unmarked in heaven. Her eyes are sweet and subtle, wild and sleepy, by turns; oftentimes rising to the clouds, oftentimes challenging the heavens. She wears a diadem round her head.    And I knew by childish memories that she could go abroad upon the winds, when she heard the sobbing of litanies or the thundering of organs, and when she beheld the mustering of summer clouds.    This sister, the eldest, it is that carries keys more than papal at her girdle, which open every cottage and every palace.    She, to my knowledge, sat all last summer by the bedside of the blind beggar, him that so often and so gladly I talked with, whose pious daughter, eight years old, with the sunny countenance, resisted the temptations of play and village mirth to travel all day long on dusty roads with her afflicted father.    For this did God send her a great reward.    In the spring time of the year, and whilst her own spring was budding, he recalled her to himself.    But her blind father mourns for ever over *her ;* still he dreams at midnight that the little guiding hand is locked within his own; and still he awakens to a darkness that is now within a second and a deeper darkness.    This *Mater Lachrymarum* also has been sitting all this winter of 1844-5 within the bedchamber of the Czar, bringing before his eyes a daughter, not less pious, that vanished to God not less suddenly, and left behind her a darkness not less profound.    By the power of the keys it is that Our Lady of Tears glides, a ghostly intruder, into the chambers of sleepless men, sleepless women, sleepless children, from Ganges to the Nile, from Nile to Mississippi.    And her, because she is the first-born of her house, and has the widest empire, let us honour with the title of Madonna.

The second sister is called *Mater Suspiriorum,* Our Lady of Sighs.    She never scales the clouds, nor walks abroad upon the winds.    She wears no diadem.    And her eyes, if they were ever seen, would be neither sweet nor subtle ; no man could read their story ; they would be found filled with perishing dreams, and with wrecks of forgotten delirium.    But she raises not her eyes ; her head, on which sits a dilapidated turban, droops for ever, for ever fastens on the dust.  She weeps not.  She groans not.  But she sighs inaudibly at intervals.  Her sister, Madonna, is oftentimes stormy and frantic, raging in the highest against heaven, and demanding back her darlings.  But Our Lady of Sighs never clamours, never defies, dreams not of rebellious aspirations.  She is humble to abjectness.  Hers is the meekness that belongs to the hopeless.  Murmur she may, but it is in her sleep.  Whisper she may, but it is to herself in the twilight.  Mutter she does at times, but it is in solitary places that are desolate as she is desolate, in ruined cities, and when the sun has gone down to his rest.  This sister is the visitor of the Pariah, of the Jew, of the bondsman to the oar in the Mediterranean galleys; of the English criminal in Norfolk Island, blotted out from the books of remembrance in sweet far-off England; of the baffled penitent reverting his eyes for ever upon a solitary grave, which to him seems the altar overthrown of some past and bloody sacrifice, on which altar no oblations can now be availing, whether towards pardon that he might implore, or towards reparation that he might attempt.  Every slave that at noonday looks up to the tropical sun with timid reproach, as he points with one hand to the earth, our general mother, but for *him* a stepmother,—as he points with the other hand to the Bible, our general teacher, but against *him* sealed and sequestered; every woman sitting in darkness, without love to shelter her head, or hope to illumine her solitude, because the heaven-born instincts kindling in her nature germs of holy affections, which God implanted in her womanly bosom, having been stifled by social necessities, now burn sullenly to waste, like sepulchral lamps amongst the ancients; every nun defrauded of her unreturning May-time by wicked kinsmen, whom God will judge; all that are betrayed, and all that are rejected; outcasts by traditionary law, and children of hereditary disgrace:—all these walk with Our Lady of Sighs.  She also carries a key, but she needs it little.  For her kingdom is chiefly amongst the tents of Shem, and the houseless vagrant of every clime.  Yet in the very highest walks of man she finds chapels of her own; and even in glorious England there are some that, to the world, carry their heads as proudly as the reindeer, who yet secretly have received her mark upon their foreheads.

But the third sister, who is also the youngest—! Hush! whisper whilst we talk of *her*! Her kingdom is not large, or else no flesh should live; but within that kingdom all power is hers. Her head, turreted like that of Cybele, rises almost beyond the reach of sight. She droops not; and her eyes, rising so high, *might* be hidden by distance. But, being what they are, they cannot be hidden; through the treble veil of crape which she wears, the fierce light of a blazing misery, that rests not for matins or for vespers, for noon of day or noon of night, for ebbing or for flowing tide, may be read from the very ground. She is the defier of God. She is also the mother of lunacies and the suggestress of suicides. Deep lie the roots of her power, but narrow is the nation that she rules. For she can approach only those in whom a profound nature has been upheaved by central convulsions, in whom the heart trembles and the brain rocks under conspiracies of tempest from without and tempest from within. Madonna moves with uncertain steps, fast or slow, but still with tragic grace. Our Lady of Sighs creeps timidly and stealthily. But this youngest sister moves with incalculable motions, bounding, and with tiger's leaps. She carries no key; for, though coming rarely amongst men, she storms all doors at which she is permitted to enter at all. And *her* name is *Mater Tenebrarum*, Our Lady of Darkness.

This is prose-poetry; but it is more. It is a permanent addition to the mythology of the human race. As the Graces are three, as the Fates are three, as the Furies are three, as the Muses were originally three, so may the varieties and degrees of misery that there are in the world, and the proportions of their distribution among mankind, be represented to the human imagination for ever by De Quincey's Three Ladies of Sorrow and his sketch of their figures and kingdoms.

# INDEX.

THE END.

*Printed by* R. & R. CLARK, LIMITED, *Edinburgh.*

# English Men of Letters.

### Edited by JOHN MORLEY.

*Popular Edition. Paper Covers, 1s. ; Cloth, 1s. 6d.*
*Library Edition. Crown 8vo. Gilt tops. Flat backs. 2s. net each.*

## NEW SERIES.

*Crown 8vo. Gilt tops. Flat backs. 2s. net each.*

MACMILLAN AND CO., LTD., LONDON.

# English Men of Action Series.

Crown 8vo. Cloth. With Portraits. 2s. 6d. each.

**CAMPBELL (COLIN).**
By ARCHIBALD FORBES.
**CLIVE.**
By Sir CHARLES WILSON.
**COOK (Captain).**
By Sir WALTER BESANT.
**DAMPIER.**
By W. CLARK RUSSELL.
**DRAKE.**
By JULIAN CORBETT.
**DUNDONALD.**
By the Hon. J. W. FORTESCUE.
**GORDON (General).**
By Sir W. BUTLER.
**HASTINGS (Warren).**
By Sir A. LYALL.
**HAVELOCK (Sir Henry).**
By A. FORBES.
**HENRY V.**
By the Rev. A. J. CHURCH.
**LAWRENCE (Lord).**
By Sir RICHARD TEMPLE.

**LIVINGSTONE.**
By THOMAS HUGHES.
**MONK.**
By JULIAN CORBETT.
**MONTROSE.**
By MOWBRAY MORRIS.
**NAPIER (Sir Charles).**
By Colonel Sir W. BUTLER.
**NELSON.**
By Prof. J. K. LAUGHTON.
**PETERBOROUGH.**
By W. STEBBING.
**RODNEY.**
By DAVID HANNAY.
**STRAFFORD.**
By H. D. TRAILL.
**WARWICK, the King-Maker.**
By C. W. OMAN.
**WELLINGTON.**
By GEORGE HOOPER.
**WOLFE.**
By A. G. BRADLEY.

# Twelve English Statesmen.

Crown 8vo. 2s. 6d. each.

\*\* *A Series of Short Biographies, not designed to be a complete roll of famous Statesmen, but to present in historic order the lives and work of those leading actors in our affairs who by their direct influence have left an abiding mark on the policy, the institutions, and the position of Great Britain among States.*

**WILLIAM THE CON-
QUEROR.** By EDWARD A. FREE-
MAN, D.C.L., LL.D., late Regius
Professor of Modern History in the
University of Oxford.
**HENRY II.**
By Mrs. J. R. GREEN.
**EDWARD I.**
By T. F. TOUT, M.A., Professor of
History, The Owens College, Man-
chester.
**HENRY VII.**
By JAMES GAIRDNER.
**CARDINAL WOLSEY.**
By Bishop CREIGHTON, D.D., late
Dixie Professor of Ecclesiastical His-
tory in the University of Cambridge.

**ELIZABETH.**
By E. S. BEESLY, M.A., Professor
of Modern History, University College,
London.
**OLIVER CROMWELL.**
By FREDERIC HARRISON.
**WILLIAM III.**
By H. D. TRAILL.
**WALPOLE.**
By JOHN MORLEY.
**CHATHAM.**
By JOHN MORLEY. [*In preparation*
**PITT.**
By Lord ROSEBERY.
**PEEL.**
By J. R. THURSFIELD, M.A., late
Fellow of Jesus College, Oxford.

MACMILLAN AND CO., LTD., LONDON.